Stop the Spiral

25 Techniques to Break Overthinking, Calm Your Nervous System, and Find Peace in the Present

Michelle Mann

Table of Contents

Introduction

You open your inbox, and emails are piling up—some marked urgent, others nagging with the promise of more work before the day is even half over. Your shoulders tense, a silent ache settling in as you try to remember if you already answered that one stressful message. Maybe you can feel your heart picking up pace, or notice your mind spiraling into a loop: Did I mess something up? What if I fall behind? This scene, in some form or another, might feel like your daily reality—racing thoughts mid-task, tension climbing during family conversations, or that deep sense of emotional overload when your calendar refuses to let up. If any part of this sounds like you, know you're not alone. I've seen it in my clients, my colleagues, and, at times, in myself.

What if there was a set of real, practical tools—rooted in science, not hype—that you could reach for in the very moments when overwhelm strikes? That's the promise of this book: every page is packed with ways to shift from feeling trapped by stress, burnout, or emotional overload to cultivating steadiness, clarity, and control. Imagine moving through your week with a toolkit you trust—setting healthy boundaries without guilt, easing the mental noise when your mind won't quit, and restoring energy for the moments (and people) that matter most. These aren't just skills for tough days—they are the foundation for a sustainable, resilient mindset you can rely on.

If you're picking up this book, chances are you've struggled with overthinking, felt burned out by relentless to-do lists, or wished for better boundaries at work and at home. Maybe you've cycled through countless self-care tips, only to feel like nothing fits your busy, layered life. Underneath it all, perhaps you worry that your emotions are "too much," fear judgment when you speak up, or carry shame about not handling it all perfectly. Maybe, like many high-achieving adults, you secretly wonder: Is it possible to actually change my patterns—or will I always be running to catch up? If so, I see you. Every fear, skepticism, and exhausted hope is welcome here.

I'm Dr. Maya Rivera, a clinical psychologist with over 15 years of experience supporting driven, creative adults who feel emotionally stretched thin. My passion is turning complex neuroscience and mind–body research into everyday tools you can use between emails, during commutes, or amid late-night worries. With advanced training in somatic therapy and trauma recovery, I blend evidence-based science with practical compassion. But I'm not just coming at this as a clinician—I've lived these pressures myself. Like you, I've navigated burnout, self-doubt, and the powerful urge to keep pushing past my limits. That's why everything in this book is designed not just to work in theory, but to fit busy, beautiful, imperfect lives like yours.

Maybe you've tried self-help books before and felt let down— by empty promises, unrealistic routines, or advice that had more judgment than empathy. Here's what makes this book different: It's part workbook, part supportive guide, written in down-to-earth language and built for real life. Here you'll find trauma-sensitive practices, inclusive examples for diverse backgrounds and identities, and digital and audio resources to make learning accessible on the go. Each chapter is crafted with care to help you feel seen, never shamed; understood, not overwhelmed.

Your journey through this book will be hands-on from the start. We'll begin by spotting and softening overthinking loops so you can interrupt stress before it takes over—learning how your body and mind work together (and sometimes against you). As you move forward, you'll practice calming techniques, micro-habits for emotional relief, flexible boundary scripts, and habit rewrites that gradually replace old cycles with healthier defaults. Expect practical exercises you can do right away, quick scripts to use in tough moments, reflection prompts to deepen your self-awareness, and habit trackers to keep your growth visible and rewarding.

You might wonder: Can I really regulate emotions in the heat of a meltdown? Is there a way to finally stop ruminating at 2AM? How do I heal from old wounds without reliving them— and when should I seek professional support? Throughout these pages, you'll find clear answers, transparent guidance, and permission to pace yourself. Whether your goal is to handle stress better at work, improve relationships, or simply find a few minutes of peace each day, I promise practical direction—with room for all your questions and doubts along the way.

Above all, this is an invitation to active transformation. Don't just read—talk back, scribble in the margins, put these tools to work in your daily life. Progress isn't about getting every exercise "right" or being perfectly calm all the time; it's about showing up, practicing kindness toward yourself, and making shifts one moment at a time. Treat this book as your companion—a toolkit, a cheerleader, and sometimes a gentle nudge—on your path toward more freedom, steadiness, and joy.

So let's begin. The first steps start now, right where you are. Chapter 1 will teach you to spot your spirals sooner and soften their impact. Relief can come quickly—even today. You're not behind, and it's not too late to reclaim your sense of calm, agency, and hope. This book is yours; let's dive in together and rewrite the story of emotional overload—starting with your next breath.

Chapter 1: Spot the Spiral: Recognize It Faster, Soften It Sooner

Imagine you're managing your investments, watching different strategies play out over time. One approach might be steady and cautious, slowly growing your portfolio with less risk. Another could be more aggressive, aiming for bigger gains but carrying the chance of sharper losses. As you watch these strategies unfold, it becomes clear how the way you react to market changes—whether sticking to a plan or spiraling into worry—can make a big difference in your outcomes. This isn't just about numbers; it's about recognizing patterns that can quietly take over your thinking and your decisions.

This chapter will explore how spotting these spirals early—like noticing early shifts in your portfolio—gives you the chance to soften their impact before they grow. We'll unpack what happens inside your mind and body during these moments, how to map your personal warning signs, and practical ways to name and tame those spirals quickly. By treating your mental loops like investment moves you can monitor and adjust, you gain more control over how stress and overthinking affect your day-to-day life.

The Overthinking Loop Explained

Picture the last time your mind wouldn't let go of a conversation replay or a work slip—just like the story in this chapter's opening scene. Your thoughts circled, your body tensed, and every new angle seemed to magnify the original worry. This isn't just being 'too sensitive' or having a personality quirk. It's the overthinking loop at work, turning ordinary stress into a runaway spiral. Understanding how this loop works takes it from feeling like a flaw to seeing it as something you can spot and shift. The power comes from recognizing that loops are predictable—and interruptible—patterns, not failures of willpower.

Cognitive Loop Mechanics

When you're awake at night replaying an awkward email or drafting ten different responses to a simple message, you've landed squarely in the cognitive loop. The brain chews through the same storylines, convinced that more thinking will solve the problem—or prevent embarrassment, rejection, or loss. Confirmation bias slides right into this mix: your mind scouts for "evidence" that supports or threatens your main fear, while ignoring any neutral or comforting facts. You might only remember the one frown during a meeting rather than all the nods. By recycling these familiar mental tracks, the system stirs up fresh anxiety, feeding itself with each pass. Disrupting the sameness—even by asking a curious new question, changing scenery, or saying your thoughts out loud—can drop a wedge in the gears of rumination (Bryant, 2021). Spotting this mechanical nature is what gives you leverage. If the process is automatic, so is your chance to interrupt it.

Stress Chemistry Snapshot

That rush of urgency you feel? It's not just mental. When a perceived threat hits—like an unresolved work message or criticism—your body shifts fast. Stress chemicals such as cortisol surge, setting off a fight-or-flight alert inside. That's why spirals can turn physical: tight shoulders, clenched jaw, pounding heart, or a fluttery stomach (Murphy et al., 2022). Under this spell, the brain moves to black-and-white thinking. You'll notice it's harder to see nuance; solutions shrink down to "fix it now or lose everything." In these moments, short physical shifts matter. Even a long exhale or uncrossing your legs pulls tiny levers on this chemistry, creating quiet space for your next move. Recognizing the physical roots of urgency helps you separate real emergencies from old alarms, rewiring your sense of control.

Attention as Velcro

Your mind was built for survival. That meant scanning for danger signals—the modern version is waiting for feedback after sending an important document or anxiously checking your phone for a reply that doesn't come. The brain acts like Velcro for possible threats, but everything else becomes Teflon; good news slips away, doubts stick stubbornly. Ever find yourself locked onto a single ambiguous text or reviewing all the ways something could go wrong? That's selective attention in action. To break this grip, simply naming present-moment sights or sounds can help widen your focus. When you look around and quietly describe the details of your room or the sound of distant traffic, your attention stretches just enough that worry loses its monopoly.

Body Leads the Mind

Before the spiral even picks up speed, early physical cues show up: maybe your breathing gets shallow before a tough call, or your jaw tightens while your inbox fills. Most people notice the mental chatter first, but the loop nearly always starts in the body (Murphy et al., 2022). These cues aren't warnings of failure—they're useful alerts. A tight neck doesn't mean you're doomed to rumination; it means you're catching the spiral at its source. Practice noticing these patterns, and you give yourself an early signal to pause or reset, fast-tracking yourself out of autopilot overthinking.

With the loop mechanics clear, the next step is to map your personal early-warning signals so you can catch spirals sooner.

Early Warning Signal Map: Your Personalized Spiral Radar

Now that the science of spirals and stress loops has come to life, it's time to translate this understanding into action. Catching a mental spiral early can keep you from being swept up in hours of worry or self-criticism. Building your early warning signal map turns self-awareness from theory into a tool you use every day. Even a little curiosity about your first signs is already a step toward more control. No one gets this perfect on the first try—think of today as the beginning of a map you can update anytime.

Body Cues Inventory

Stress often shows up in the body before thoughts or actions catch up. A quick body scan—from head to toe—can shine a spotlight on your personal warning lights. Some people feel tension between their eyes or tightness in their jaw. Others notice that their chest feels hot or hands start to go cold. Let's get curious. Here are ten common cues to look for:
- Frown lines or furrowed brows
- Jaw tightness
- Throat constriction
- Shallow breathing
- Heart beating faster

- Stomach clenching
- Cold hands or feet
- Shoulders pulling up near ears
- Chest heat or pressure
- Restlessness or jittery limbs

Put a checkmark next to those you experience most. Add any unique to you—some people feel itchy skin or a buzzing scalp. Keep this list in your phone or journal so you can spot the first flickers of stress as they appear (George, 2024).

Thought Triggers List

Before overthinking takes over, signature thoughts often pop up. These thought patterns act like storm warnings for mental spirals. Common examples include:
- "What if I mess this up?"
- "They'll think I'm incompetent."
- "I have to fix this now."
- "I'm falling behind."

Take a moment to jot down your frequent starters. Now group them into themes like perfectionism, approval-seeking, control, or fear of uncertainty. Maybe you notice these thoughts come up late at night, before big meetings, or during quiet moments at home. Note when and where yours tend to flare. Spotting these patterns makes them less mysterious and easier to interrupt (jeremyp, 2024).

Behavior Flags

Actions often wave red flags before our feelings catch up with them. Some people doom-scroll without thinking. Others open five browser tabs, re-read an email for the third time, or obsessively check notifications. Rather than seeing these behaviors as failures, call them your built-in alarms—they're not good or bad, just information. Write down your top two or three behaviors that show up early in a spiral. Put reminders near common traps—a sticky note that says "Pause?" on your laptop, or a five-minute timer on your phone when scrolling social feeds. Noticing these patterns is a win in itself. Everyone does some version of them; noticing is all that matters (jeremyp, 2024).

Intensity Scale

Once you have your signal list, bring in an intensity scale to make sense of how things build. Use a simple 1–5 range:
1 – Slight shift, like mild tension
2 – Noticeable but manageable
3 – Clearly agitated or distracted
4 – Feeling out of control
5 – Overwhelmed or panicked

Mark your personal pivot point—the level where you can still step in before the spiral runs away with itself. For many, a "2" or "3" is that window. For example, if stomach clenching reaches level 3, pause for a reset. Track your ratings throughout a week. Over time, you'll see how fast things move from mild to urgent, and you can plan fast relief steps accordingly (George, 2024; jeremyp, 2024).

Making It Yours—and What's Next

Give yourself space to experiment. If your first attempt at mapping feels off, try again tomorrow. There's no scorecard here—every spark of awareness counts. Those who feel more in their body may fill out the physical cues first, while thought-oriented readers may keep more detailed trigger lists. You might spot your signature behaviors while working late or parenting through bedtime chaos. Every person's map is unique, and each attempt grows your self-knowledge.

The purpose of mapping isn't to avoid stress altogether—it's to give yourself the earliest signals possible, so you have more choices. Even if you catch just one sign today, that's progress worth celebrating. Once you can spot and rate your cues, you're ready to use a fast, science-backed tool: naming what you feel. This practice will help you step out of the spiral with more confidence and control.

Why Naming It Helps

Now that you've mapped your early warning signals, here's why pausing to name what you feel can make a difference. Labeling your emotions is more than just putting a word to a feeling—it's a fast way to turn down the alarm system in your brain and help you step out of the spiral. When stress or frustration starts to build, your amygdala—your brain's internal smoke detector—flares up. This part kicks off fast, automatic reactions: you snap at your partner, fire off a tense email, or replay one mistake again and again. The act of saying (out loud or silently), "I'm anxious," or "I notice tension," dials down this response. Just naming the emotion sends a signal to your brain that you're paying attention; it's almost like talking to a child who's throwing a tantrum by calmly describing what you see. Even a brief pause to say, "I'm angry," as your jaw clenches after reading a tough email can take the edge off, buying you a little space to respond with more choice (Burklund et al., 2014).

Putting feelings into words does something else, too; it shifts gears from raw emotion to problem-solving mode. That's your prefrontal cortex—right behind your forehead—kicking in. Instead of being hijacked by loops of dread or irritation, naming what's happening gives you back a steering wheel. For example, if your chest tightens and thoughts start racing before a team meeting, saying, "This is nervousness about the meeting" turns a vague wall of anxiety into something clear you can work with. With that bit of clarity, new solutions are possible—maybe jotting down some ideas to prepare, stepping outside for a minute, or re-reading your goals. You move from overwhelm toward action (Burklund et al., 2014).

Naming works best when it's precise. Vague labels like "bad" or "off" leave you stuck without a plan. Pinning down whether you feel "irritated" or "worried" matters because it shapes your next move. If you realize you're irritated, it might mean you need to set a boundary, close your office door, or ask for more time. If it's sadness, comfort or connection might be the real fix. You build a kind of emotional toolkit this way—the bigger your vocabulary, the easier it is to spot and diffuse spirals next time. Noticing patterns over days or weeks, such as always feeling "restless" on Sunday nights, opens the door to new habits or boundaries.

The language you use when labeling feelings acts like a lever. Choosing first-person, present tense—phrases like "I notice overwhelm" or "I feel anger rising"—transforms self-talk from judgment to observation. Try ones like, "This is just stress," or "I'm noticing embarrassment right now." These little scripts are gentle cues that your emotions are states, not personal failings. This approach normalizes having all kinds of feelings, giving you a buffer before acting out old habits. Imagine standing in front of the fridge after a taxing day, and instead of eating mindlessly, you quietly say, "I notice I'm worn out and searching for comfort." This moment of awareness creates a pause—a crack where you might choose a walk, a glass of water, or calling a friend instead of reacting automatically (Burklund et al., 2014; Yoshimura et al., 2022).

Affect labeling works on both neural activity and everyday behavior. Brain research shows it reduces the intensity of distress signals in the amygdala while boosting involvement from regions that support reasoning and control (Burklund et al., 2014; Yoshimura et al., 2022). What matters for overloaded adults is that this isn't just theory. Naming emotions works in busy homes, tense offices, or any place you get triggered. Some people worry that focusing on feelings will make them worse, but study after study finds the opposite— naming what's true helps you calm your body and sharpens your thinking. After mapping your warning signals, let's unpack what shifts when you actually put your feelings into words. With the science in mind, you're ready to try a 60-second practice to put naming into action.

Apply Now: Name It to Tame It

All the science and strategies from earlier have set you up perfectly for real-life practice. With your brain already primed by what you've just learned, this exercise walks you through a fast, repeatable way to step out of an emotional spiral. You'll use it whenever the day runs off track or your mind starts to swirl. You don't need fancy tools or lots of time—just one minute, a bit of curiosity, and willingness to try. Here's how to do it.

30-Second Scan

Begin by reassuring yourself that these next steps aren't meant to pressure you or demand perfection. Set a timer for 30 seconds. If you're comfortable, close your eyes; if not, rest your gaze softly in front of you. Let yourself notice three different body sensations. These might be obvious—"my fists are clenched," "there's a knot in my stomach." Or they could be subtle—"my hands feel cool after typing," "my foot is tapping," "the right side of my jaw tingles." Describe each sensation with both a location and the quality. For example: "left shoulder, heavy and tight; palms, dry and tingly; belly, fluttery." Your only job is to pay attention, not to change anything. If nothing pops out, that's fine—sometimes noticing the absence of feeling teaches just as much. Curiosity is your only goal here, not correctness. Even if your thoughts wander, return gently to asking, "what am I actually feeling?"

Emotion Label

Next, bring your focus to whatever feels most intense or pronounced. From what you noticed, ask yourself, "What emotion is closest to the surface right now?" Pick one— sadness, irritation, worry, guilt, numbness, restlessness. If none fit, make up your own label or combine words. Give it a number between 1 and 10, where 1 is almost gone and 10 is overwhelming. Practice saying quietly to yourself, "I'm feeling [emotion] at about a [number]," for instance, "I'm feeling edgy at about a 6," or "There's heaviness—a 4." The task here isn't to pinpoint why or debate accuracy—one short sentence does the trick. There's no need to overthink or write a long entry. Trust that this act of naming is enough to shift your mental gears (Torre & Lieberman, 2018).

If finding a word is tough, try using a color, temperature, or energy level—"gray and slow," "hot and urgent." Naming whatever comes helps your brain move out of fight-or-flight and into clarity. If more than one emotion shows up, pick the one that feels strongest or most distracting. Remind yourself: it's normal for new feelings to pop up as you pay attention. There are no wrong answers.

Anchor Phrase

Pause here for an anchor. Say aloud or to yourself, "A wave, not a verdict." Pair this with a longer exhale than usual, letting your breath out slowly. Picture emotions like weather—they come and go, but never define who you are. Imagine waiting at a red light. Annoying, maybe, but always temporary. This phrase interrupts the urge to judge, panic, or fix anything quickly. If you feel silly, that's expected for something new. The point is to shift from urgency to acceptance, even for a moment.

Recheck

Now scan inward again for another 20 or 30 seconds. Notice if your emotion's intensity changed. Maybe that 6 drops to a 5, or just shifts in quality—"less prickly, more dull." Any movement counts. Say, "If my number dropped, that's my nervous system resetting. Well done." If it stayed the same, that's also normal. Sometimes relief comes in waves, sometimes not yet. In those cases, loop back and try the script again, or add a favorite grounding technique like squeezing a stress ball or taking a slow sip of water.

End by deciding what's next. If there's some relief, move forward with your day. If things still feel stuck, stack this routine with another tool—you're building a toolbox, not passing a test. Keep track of when and where this script works best by making a few notes during your week. Over time, you'll see patterns and feel more confident interrupting spirals before they get bigger.

Remember, each time you pause to name and rate your feelings—even if awkward or incomplete—you're building self-awareness, teaching your brain to use words instead of rumination, and giving yourself a chance to reset before overwhelm takes over (Torre & Lieberman, 2018; Wadlinger & Isaacowitz, 2010; *No Rules Just Write: A New Approach to Journaling*, 2025).

Wrapping Up

It's easy to get caught in those mental loops where stress builds and our minds race over the same thoughts again and again. This chapter was all about understanding how overthinking works, recognizing the early cues—whether they show up in your body, your thoughts, or your behaviors—and learning simple ways to interrupt that cycle. By mapping your own warning signals and practicing naming what you feel, you're giving yourself better odds at stepping out of spirals before they take over your day.

Every time you pause to check in with your body and name your emotions, you're building new habits that turn self-awareness into an everyday tool. These strategies don't erase life's pressures, but they do help you meet them with a little less overwhelm and a bit more clarity. Keep experimenting with the cues and techniques that fit you best. Each small step is a win, and you'll find that breaking free from the overthinking loop gets easier each time you practice.

Chapter 2: Box Breathing Reset: Calm the Body, Quiet the Mind

Your phone buzzes again: an urgent email pops up with the subject line, "Need revisions by EOD." Your chest tightens instantly, the weight of pressure pulling your shoulders up toward your ears. Suddenly, your mind floods with questions—What did I overlook? How can I fix this quickly? You feel scattered, overwhelmed, caught in a mental storm where panic threatens to take over. But instead of reacting immediately, you pause. You set a 90-second timer on your phone, plant both feet firmly on the floor beneath you, and begin to breathe intentionally, tracing an invisible square through your breath: inhaling for four counts, holding for four, exhaling for four, then pausing again for four. As you continue this simple cycle, the tension in your jaw slowly releases, your heartbeat drifts into a calmer rhythm, and the noise in your mind quiets down. That stressful email feels a little less daunting. Your response forms with clarity, not chaos.

This chapter invites you to explore how something as basic as your breath can become a powerful tool to shift your body's state from alarm to calm whenever stress hits. Breath is like a remote control for your nervous system—at your fingertips anytime you need it. We'll break down why controlling this natural reflex helps reset your internal balance and offers a steady anchor amid daily overwhelm. Then, you'll learn exactly how to harness the box breathing technique so that when life demands you stay cool under fire, you have a practical, discreet method ready to bring you back to center—no matter where you are or how frantic things get.

Breath as a Remote Control

After untangling how spirals hijack body and mind, it helps to see why breath stands out as your first reliable reset tool. The body is hardwired so breath and nervous system always check in with each other. Fast, shallow panting can make your heart race and send out alarms, while slow, regular breathing tells the body it's time to calm down (Russo et al., 2017). You don't have to believe in it for the effect to work—any shift in breath pattern changes the signals sent from lungs and chest muscles to the brain. Ever caught yourself sighing with relief after tough news passes? That exhale is your nervous system's way of confirming safety.

Breathe in, breathe out—the cycle never stops. But not all breaths are created equal. The pace you keep, not how much air you gulp, is what matters most under stress. Picture yourself at a red light or in a meeting: rapid, shallow breaths can fuel tension. Slow, even breaths act like a volume knob, lowering the background noise of anxiety. The nervous system listens closely, tuning its activity to match. When you draw air in quietly, pause, then let a long exhale slip out, you train your stress controls to dial back alarm levels immediately (Birdee et al., 2023; Russo et al., 2017).

Now consider your heartbeat. Scientists call its moment-to-moment change "heart rate variability"—it's not as scary as it sounds. Imagine your breath as a metronome; every smooth inhale-exhale sequence gently guides your heartbeat into a steadier rhythm. This sync between heart and breath doesn't just look good on a chart. It means you move from scattered and frazzled toward a state where you handle feedback with less sting or recall details under pressure. The more smoothly your heart responds to your breath, the easier it is to reset focus mid-afternoon instead of spiraling into brain fog (Russo et al., 2017).

Slow isn't just a suggestion. The research points to slow-paced breathing—somewhere in the ballpark of five to seven breaths per minute—as a sweet spot for calming the body without needing extra effort or equipment (Russo et al., 2017). This isn't about deep, dramatic gasps that leave you lightheaded. It's about gentle pacing that you can use at a stoplight, before opening your inbox, or riding the elevator. When the rhythm is steady and unforced, signals from your lungs and diaphragm reach hubs in your brain in charge of stress and focus, helping you handle chaos with a little more grace (Birdee et al., 2023).

Breath has one more trick up its sleeve: the exhale. Drawing out your out-breath is like finding the brake pedal in the middle of a busy day. During that long exhale, the "rest and digest" arm of your nervous system—the vagus nerve—gets dialed up. This process, called boosting "vagal tone," helps lower your heart rate and relaxes tensions in places like your jaw or shoulders. Think of letting air out through pursed lips as gently easing off the gas when traffic slows. Over time, practicing longer exhales makes this stress brake easier to tap even on hectic Mondays or before tough conversations (Russo et al., 2017).

Changing your breathing might feel too simple at first glance. Yet every physical cue—from your heartbeat to muscle tightness—responds to these tiny shifts. Breath patterns work not because they trick you but because your nervous system is wired to listen. By giving yourself a reliable way to lower the inner noise, you move from feeling hijacked by stress toward having a dial you can actually turn.

With the 'why' in place, next up is the 'how'—a step-by-step guide you can use right away. So far, we've mapped out the problem; now we're collecting hands-on solutions. Having unpacked why breath is a remote control for your stress response, let's walk through exactly what to do—no guessing required.

(Russo et al., 2017; Birdee et al., 2023)

Technique Blueprint: 4x4x4x4

Box breathing is more than a trendy tool—it's one of the simplest and most reliable ways to interrupt the body's stress alarm and return your system to steady. For high-achieving, busy adults juggling work, family, and personal goals, having a technique you can use discreetly anywhere (at your desk, in the car, before a meeting) is crucial. This section gives you clear, step-by-step instructions for practicing the 4x4x4x4 box breathing method, so you can install calm in real life—not just when you're alone on a yoga mat.

Before you start, remember that this exercise is built on science-backed breathing patterns proven to lower stress hormones, steady heart rate, and activate your body's relaxation response (Stinson, 2024; Gotter, 2020). Whether you're new to breathwork or have some experience with mindfulness practices, these steps are designed to be approachable for all fitness levels. If you need to modify any element (shorter holds, supported posture), that's absolutely fine—comfort comes first.

Box Breathing (4x4x4x4)

Target areas: Diaphragm, lungs, nervous system regulation
Difficulty: Beginner
Duration: 2–5 minutes (start shorter if needed)
Steps:
1. Find a seat where your back is supported and both feet rest flat on the floor. Imagine a string gently lengthening your spine upward while letting your shoulders drop down and back. Wiggle your jaw side to side, then let it relax. Rest your tongue gently on the roof of your mouth behind your upper teeth to encourage nasal breathing.
2. Place your hands palm-down on your thighs or on your desk. Lower your gaze softly or close your eyes halfway— this helps reduce distractions. Some people like to focus

their eyes on a neutral point or trace a square in their mind as they breathe.

3. Start the rhythm: Inhale slowly through your nose to a silent count of 1-2-3-4, feeling air fill your lower ribs and belly. Hold your breath softly at the top for another 1-2-3-4. Exhale gently out through your nose or mouth for 1-2-3-4, feeling your ribs descend and tension leave the body. Hold again at the bottom for 1-2-3-4 before starting the next inhale.

4. Repeat this cycle for four full rounds. Notice how your chest, shoulders, and jaw soften with each round. Keep the breath smooth—never forced or held to the point of discomfort. If holding your breath feels tense, skip the holds or shorten the count to three seconds per phase instead.

5. Need a modification? If you become lightheaded or uneasy, switch to a 3-3-3-3 pattern or use a "hold-free" approach: inhale 4, exhale 4, repeat. If fidgety, gently press thumb and index finger together as you count each segment—this anchors attention and eases restlessness.

Form cues:
- Sit tall but not rigid; avoid craning the neck or clenching the abs.
- Relax your jaw, face, and belly as much as possible.
- Breathe quietly—soundless is ideal, but soft audible breaths are okay if soothing.
- Always prioritize ease over strict form; no gold medals for perfect counts!

Tips and common mistakes to avoid:
- Don't force full, deep inhales if your chest feels tight—let your breath flow naturally at its easiest depth.
- Avoid holding your breath beyond comfort. Feeling edgy or dizzy? Shorten the count or skip the holds altogether.
- Keep your shoulders soft. If they start creeping toward your ears, pause and let them drop before resuming.

This simple protocol preps your body for greater emotional steadiness by teaching your nervous system how to shift from 'threat' to 'safe.' With practice, you'll notice it gets easier and more natural—and you won't need perfect conditions to feel results. On tough days, even two cycles can make a measurable difference.

In the next section, you'll learn how to apply this exact technique in urgent, everyday moments—like before sending a heated email or during a stressful commute—using a fast 90-second reset and clever habit hacks.

Apply Now: 90-Second Rescue

You've learned the blueprint for box breathing and how to set your posture. Now it's time to bring this into daily life—not in a quiet room, but right in the middle of real-world messiness. Practicing box breathing isn't only about sitting cross-legged with your eyes closed; it's about having a short reset you can use while racing to meetings, caught in traffic, or staring down a tense email. Each time you reach for this skill, you're giving your mind and body a short, clear signal: it's safe to steady down for a moment. That's progress.

Try out these quick resets, tailored for the moments you actually need them:

Micro-Set: The 90-Second Space

Imagine your pulse is up and you're about to send a high-stakes message or answer a tough question. Here's how to use box breathing as a mini reset:
1. Set a timer for 60 to 90 seconds on your phone.
2. Plant both feet flat. Sit or stand tall—shoulders easy.
3. Inhale through your nose for four counts. Hold for four. Exhale for four. Pause for four. Repeat this pattern four times (or until the timer ends).
4. As you finish, notice if your jaw unclenches, your shoulders drop, or thoughts come in a bit softer. If you feel dizzy, shorten the breath or skip the holds—comfort comes first.

Chances are, words flow a little easier after. Your reply might feel less tight or rushed. Even a brief break lets your brain move from panic to focus, boosting agency over reactions (Balban et al., 2023).

Silent Counting & Finger Taps

Let's say you're stuck in a meeting, public place, or somewhere that feels awkward for obvious breathing exercises. You can keep things private:

1. Rest your hands gently on your lap. For each part of the box breath—inhale, hold, exhale, hold—silently count "one, two, three, four" while tapping each finger against your thumb.
2. Keep mouth closed; breathe through your nose if possible.
3. Run through this box two or three times. No one needs to know you're doing it.

This subtle approach helps you stay grounded when speaking up feels hard or nerves start buzzing in your body.

Trigger Linking: Anchor Breathing to Stress Cues

Everyday life hands us dozens of reminders to pause. Use these as anchors for your new reset skill. Try these ideas:

- Take three box breaths before hitting "send" on any stressful email.
- Practice one round at every red light, or while waiting in line for coffee.
- Link box breathing with calendar alerts: add a note to your meeting reminder, or stash a sticky note on your laptop with a tiny box drawn on it.

These habits help you call up calm exactly when you'd normally spiral into stress. Over time, your body starts making the association automatically, shrinking gaps between stress spike and self-regulation (Balban et al., 2023).

Outcome Check: Noticing Progress in Real Time

To build confidence in this practice, check in before and after you use it. Here's a way to chart your shift:

1. Before starting the box breath, ask yourself, "How tense am I?" Rate it out of 10 in your head or jot a number on a sticky note (zero: fully relaxed, ten: wound tight).
2. Do one to two minutes of box breathing in your chosen style.
3. Rate your tension again. Look for even a small drop—a point or two is a win. Jot down a word or phrase about what feels lighter.

Some days the change jumps out—your heart slows, thoughts clear. Other days are quieter, but each attempt teaches your system calm can be called up on demand. If nothing budges, that doesn't mean failure. This is skill-building, not pass/fail—consider it data.

Box breathing works because it shifts your nervous system toward balance, even in the midst of busy routines (Bentley et al., 2023; Balban et al., 2023). It's normal for some situations to require tweaks or alternatives. If anything felt tricky or didn't land perfectly, the next part offers fixes to help you find your groove with this practice.

Troubleshooting & Variations: Making Box Breathing Work for Your Body and Life

If you tried the last box breathing exercise and found it uncomfortable or tricky, you're not alone. Every body reacts a little differently—sometimes breath holds feel too intense, or stuffy noses get in the way. There's no need to force the standard method when gentle adjustments can open up this tool for everyone. This section is your guide to making box breathing match your needs, whether you're dealing with anxiety, physical challenges, or tight schedules.

Some readers find that holding their breath triggers more tension instead of calm. If that sounds familiar, try the hold-free option. Skip the pauses and use a simple 4-count inhale, followed by a longer 6-count exhale, letting each out-breath be steady but easy. Imagine this as training wheels for your breath practice. You might try a cycle like this: breathe in for four counts, breathe out for six, repeat for a few rounds. Give yourself permission to do just this if it feels best. Later, if you want, experiment by adding just a tiny pause—a gentle count of one—between breaths. Start where comfort lives. Every session counts, and even without traditional holds, you're still getting the benefits of nervous system reset (Bentley et al., 2023; Fincham et al., 2023). To track how you're doing, jot down how you feel after each session in a notebook or phone app; look for small shifts, such as feeling less jittery or regaining focus after a tough meeting.

Nasal breathing offers powerful calming effects, naturally warming and filtering air. Still, allergies or sinus pressure can make exclusive nose breathing a struggle. No need to power through discomfort or worry about breaking the rules. If nasal passages are blocked, let a bit of air flow through parted lips, or switch to mouth breathing when needed. For instance, on days when spring allergies hit hard, you might breathe in gently through both nose and mouth, then return to nasal breathing once clear. The method should serve you—not the other way around. Notice which approach makes breathing steadier and keeps effort low. A quick check-in after each practice—"Was that easier? Did I feel calmer or more tense?"—will help you fine-tune what works best for your body.

Time is tight for high-achievers, and sometimes even five minutes of structured practice feels like a stretch. It's perfectly fine to go shorter. Begin with a two-minute round of breathing—set a timer, and finish when it goes off. Only add thirty seconds every couple of days if the entire cycle stays smooth and delivers at least some ease or clarity. This gradual ramp-up removes pressure and lowers the risk of frustration or giving up. You might mark sessions off on a sticky note, calendar, or checklist app. Noticing a row of checkmarks builds visible evidence that you're showing up for yourself, even when routines are busy or messy. Each mark is proof of your investment in change, not perfection.

Physical setting matters more than most people think. External distractions and physical strain can turn a relaxing technique into another source of stress. Try experimenting with location—choose a room with cooler air, softer lighting, or extra back support, using a chair, cushion, or leaning against a wall. Adjusting your posture or propping up your feet might notice instantly less jaw clenching or shoulder tension. These tweaks aren't cheating; they're signals of care for your own nervous system. After each experiment, ask, "Did this spot make the practice easier? Was my mind clearer, or did my body settle faster?" Log your discoveries so you can recreate helpful settings next time.

Everyone's journey looks different, and some days will work better than others. Discomfort, distraction, or even mild panic during early sessions isn't failure—it's feedback. That feedback tells you what adjustments could help next time. Self-compassion is your best asset here. Instead of judging yourself, praise each attempt at skill-building, no matter the outcome. Every modified breath, every minute spent, and every self-check adds up over time to build the habit and lower the power of stress triggers (Fincham et al., 2023).

Now that you've found the personalized version that matches today's needs, pick two times for tomorrow to try it again. Maybe before opening your laptop, or right before a commute. Locking in these mini-sessions builds confidence and makes the new pattern stick. Soon, you'll start to see how adaptable breathing shapes a lasting, flexible stress reset that fits your life.

Wrapping Up

Taking a moment to breathe might seem too simple in the face of real stress, but this chapter has shown how powerful that small pause can be. Your breath truly acts as a remote control for your body's alarm system—helping you move from panic to focus in less than two minutes. With each gentle inhale and smooth exhale, you're training your nervous system to respond, not just react, no matter what chaos is swirling around you. Whether you use box breathing at your desk, in traffic, or before hitting send on a tough message, these short resets add up and start to become second nature.

Remember, there's no perfect way to do this. The point isn't to follow every step exactly, but to find what fits into your own routine and comfort. Maybe you need to skip the breath holds some days, or adjust the count when things feel off. Every attempt counts, and every bit of awareness builds momentum toward steadier days. As you practice, you'll notice shifts—not just in tense moments, but in everyday life. You're giving yourself an easy, science-backed way to take charge of stress, one breath at a time.

Chapter 3: 5-4-3-2-1 Grounding: Return to the Room

If thinking your way out of anxiety worked, you wouldn't be reading this right now. It's common to try reasoning with anxious thoughts—going over all the reasons you're safe, convincing yourself the worst won't happen, or battling endless what-ifs in your mind. But when anxiety hits hard, this logical part of your brain tends to shut down, leaving only an alarm system that's sounding loudly. Trying to debate or argue when your brain is flooded by stress feels like shouting into a storm—it rarely changes how you feel and can even make things worse.

That's where the senses come in. Instead of wrestling with racing thoughts, turning your attention to what you can see, touch, hear, smell, and taste grounds you back in the moment. This simple shift calms your nervous system more quickly because it speaks directly to your body's safety signals. In this chapter, we'll explore why focusing on sensory details works better than thought battles and walk through a practical five-step grounding method that helps you return to the room—right now, wherever you are.

Grounding Beats Rumination: Why Senses Work Better Than Thought Debates During Emotional Overload

As you may have noticed from earlier chapters, the urge to debate or outthink anxious, spiraling thoughts feels almost automatic in moments of overwhelm. You might remember scenes where you tried listing reasons not to worry or rehearsing counterarguments against every "what if," only to end up more exhausted, still circling the same loop. This kind of mental tug-of-war leaves your body on high alert and your mind tangled. The pattern is familiar—your attention sticks to problems, and each rescue thought pulls you deeper into the spiral. Now that we've mapped the spiral's traps and shown how hard it is to reason with a brain flooded by stress, it's time for a different approach.

Grounding steps away from this cycle. Instead of wrestling with your mind, it invites you to change channels—to shift your attention from noisy thoughts to immediate sensory detail. This isn't just distraction; it's a practical, science-backed way to calm the nervous system fast (Health, 2025). When you name what you see, feel, or hear, your focus moves out of the storm. It becomes about the exact color of the mug in your hand or the steady hum of a heater under your desk. Ever tried to talk yourself out of panic and ended up chasing your tail? Now imagine pausing to notice the cool ceramic against your palm or the light catching dust in a sunbeam. This simple action tethers you to the present, cutting through mental clutter. Attention has only so many resources—it can't run endless loops and monitor real world cues at full volume. By consciously naming sensations, you redirect those resources toward the concrete, giving your overworked thinking brain a break.

No debate is needed for grounding to work. If logic got you out of every anxious state, white-knuckling arguments in your head would bring relief. Yet, most people find that willpower and mental strength do little once anxiety surges. Grounding sidesteps the need to prove or disprove any thought. Your mind may still churn out scary possibilities, but the act of tuning in to the feeling of soft fabric or listening to ambient street sounds offers its own relief. Picture this: you're caught in a flurry of 'what ifs' before a big meeting. Arguing with yourself to "just calm down" only fuels the fire. But shifting focus—really noticing the temperature of the cup you hold or the rhythm of your breath—lets your system disengage from rumination without demanding certainty or perfect answers.

Sensory cues bring safety signals straight to the body. When you scan the room for five things you can see or focus on the texture of your chair, you deliver clear, neutral data to the nervous system that contradicts feelings of threat (Health, 2025). These inputs don't have to be special or dramatic: sunlight glancing off your desk, the grain of wood beneath your fingers, a distant dog barking outside a window. Every ordinary detail helps update the alarm center in your brain, communicating that nothing dangerous is happening now.

With enough repetition, this practice retrains your body to recognize safety even as old thought patterns threaten to pull you back into the spiral.

Regulation follows a body-first path. Neuroscience shows that the brain's physiological systems—the parts wired for basic safety—kick in long before logical reasoning returns after a stress spike (Barrett, 2009; Tiba, 2024). Trying to settle a racing mind with facts alone is like telling a car alarm to quiet itself while the sensors are still triggered. During a swirl of worry at your desk, try pressing both feet flat to the floor or tracing a tiny circle on the surface with one finger. Often, clarity begins to arrive after you anchor your body, not before. That's why micro-actions like listing three colors in your room or touching something cool can unlock mental breathing room that wasn't there moments ago.

Let's put this side by side: battling anxious thoughts rarely brings quick peace—half an hour later, the worries may remain, only stronger. On the other hand, imagine catching yourself mid-spiral, tapping your fingertips together, and noticing the rhythm. A minute passes. The storm in your chest eases. No argument won, but safety restored. This is the difference between fighting and redirecting.

To show how quickly this shift can work, let's compare a failed thought debate to a one-minute sensory redirect—then, we'll try the step-by-step method together. Let's move from 'why' to 'how' with the five-step sensory sweep.

Step-by-Step Sensory Sweep

When anxious thoughts take over, trying to argue with your mind rarely helps. The more you negotiate or debate, the more tangled you feel. Attention is a simple but powerful tool that can break this loop—shifting your focus from mental chatter to what's right around you. You've learned about why this works in theory; now it's time to practice together and see how grounding gives your attention a job it can actually finish.

Five Things You Can See

Look around the space, wherever you are—desk, kitchen, subway, waiting room. Notice five different things you can see. These don't have to be special or interesting. Start with whatever draws your gaze: a blue book spine, a chipped coffee mug, soft light on your wall. Let your eyes move slowly from object to object. Name each one out loud or in your mind.

- Matte black mug
- Glossy tile floor
- Wrinkled gray sweater
- Sunshine on the window
- Your phone case
  If vision feels tricky or you're somewhere dark, use other qualities: shadows, lines, shapes, or contrasts—like "light," "dark," "smooth," "rough." Pause for a breath after each

one. This slow pace encourages your mind and body to sync up for a moment.

Four Things You Can Feel

Now bring awareness to touch. You can stay still or move a bit. Try pressing your feet into the ground or chair. Notice your palm on your thigh, the softness of your sleeve, the coolness of a table. Rub your fingers together, let your hand rest on a nearby object, or squeeze a pillow. If numbness or tension shows up, that's okay. There's no wrong way to notice. List them as you go:

- Chair under my legs
- Sleeve brushing my wrist
- Fingertips tapping each other
- Cool tabletop beneath my hand
  If you only find two or three, move forward once you feel ready. The point is contact, not perfection. Each small act of noticing is a reset for your nervous system.

Three Things You Can Hear

Close your eyes, if it feels comfortable. Be curious about the sounds around you. There are usually layers: near (your own breathing or keyboard), middle (conversation in another room or hallway hum), far (traffic outside or a bird call). Don't force it. Just listen. Invite the noises to come to you instead of chasing them down.

- The whirr of your laptop
- Soft click of a pen
- Wind against the glass
  If the space is quiet, pick up on tiny details—your clothing rustling, tongue tapping teeth, even the gentle sound of your own exhale. No item is too small. Let each sound land, then take a breath before moving on.

Two Things You Can Smell

Bring your attention to scent. Take a subtle sniff of the air. Maybe you catch the smell of coffee, soap, your shirt, or the page of a book. Sometimes scents are faint or hard to name, and that's alright. Just breathe in and see if anything comes up. If nothing stands out, try getting close to something nearby— your skin, fabric, or even your own hands.

- The mild scent of laundry detergent on your sleeve
- Lingering coffee aroma on your desk
  If today isn't a scented day, simply focus on taking two slow, steady inhales and notice the feeling of airflow through your nose. Breathing itself counts as connecting to the present moment.

One Thing You Can Taste

Finish by focusing on taste. Maybe you have a sip of water, a mint, or just notice the leftover flavor in your mouth. You might lick your lips or run your tongue over your teeth. What does it feel like? Chalky, sweet, sour, nothing at all? That counts too.

- Cool water lingering on your tongue
  Even if you don't sense a strong taste, paying attention is still practicing the skill. There's nothing required for this step except willingness to check in.

Take a gentle pause. Breathe out. Notice any shift, however small—a looser jaw, steadier inhale, or a tiny drop in heart rate. Even one round of this exercise can make the edges of anxiety less sharp. If you lost track along the way, that's alright. Return to any step you remember. With this routine, attention isn't fighting anxiety—it's giving your mind and body a path forward. Next, you'll see how this tool can travel with you through meetings, commutes, and nighttime wake-ups, helping you weave these steps into the fabric of your day without fuss or pressure.

Apply Now: On-the-Go Grounding

You've just learned the basics of the sensory sweep—now is the time to help your brain use grounding when and where it matters most. Building this practice into daily life may feel strange at first, but moving from theory to action is how these skills really take root (Sutton, 2022). Life rarely pauses for ideal conditions, so practicing grounding methods in real-time gives you a fair shot at easing tough moments wherever stress shows up.

Transit can be a breeding ground for anxious thoughts and physical tension. Bodies crowd close, noise rises and falls, and your mind can start running wild. Start small: fix your eyes on one clear edge—a window frame, seat handle, or advertisement—tracing its outline with your gaze. Move a finger gently along a zipper pull or tote strap, feeling every bump or groove. Count five different things you see, four textures you can touch, three noises you notice, two smells— maybe perfume or metal—and one taste, even if it's just stale air. If there's no room to move your hand, press your foot down inside your shoe and name what you feel: sock seam, cool leather, pressure against your toes. Speaking these details silently to yourself can break a mental loop. Each sensory checkpoint acts as an anchor back to the present. Progress feels like tension dropping a notch, shoulders settling, or realizing your jaw isn't as tight. Stress on transit is common; this is only practice, not performance (Sutton, 2022).

At a desk, workplace demands stack up until every muscle tenses, especially across shoulders and neck. Use your hands as tools for coming back to the moment without drawing attention. Place one fingertip on the raised letter of a keyboard key. Feel the difference between that flat plastic and your skin. Wrap both hands around a warm mug or water bottle, letting the temperature seep through. Drag your palm once across the surface of your notebook, noticing any ridges or the coolness of a pen clip. Finally, put both feet flat on the floor and press down briefly. Drop your shoulders and lengthen one breath out. These tiny moments matter— noticing even a gentle sigh escape, pulse slowing, or eyelids blink slower—that's proof that something shifted.

Nighttime often invites a swirl of worries that stick around. Lying in bed, bring your attention to where your heels meet the mattress. Feel their weight. Next, scan slowly up to your toes, labeling each subtle sensation—softness, cool sheets, aching muscles. Inhale for three, then breathe out for five. Repeat this cycle for five rounds, trying to let the bed carry your body's weight. If thoughts keep picking up speed, say "here" or "safe" quietly or in your mind during each out-breath. Even if calm doesn't arrive all at once, half a notch of release counts. If sleep still plays hard to get, just the act of steady breathing and gentle attention soothes the system and helps prepare the mind for rest (Sutton, 2022; Macaulay et al., 2022).

Sometimes privacy disappears, whether you're at the store, standing in line, or caught at a crowded event. There's always a way to go inward. Mentally note colors or shapes in your immediate area. Use the pads of your fingers to tap out the 5-4-3-2-1 sequence inside your pocket or along your leg. If your hands stay busy or visible, slow your blinking while observing nearby sounds, giving your mind a moment of pause. Remind yourself internally—"I'm doing enough; I can try again later." No step loses power by staying quiet or private. What matters is the presence you offer yourself—for a heartbeat, a single inhale, a smile that stays just for you.

Every attempt, whether clumsy or split-second, trains your brain for next time. Expect that some days will flow better than others. The smallest shift counts as growth—remember, nobody gets calmer by judging themselves for struggling. These moments are little acts of self-kindness, building groundwork for bigger change over time (Sutton, 2022). Once you've tried adapting grounding to your own daily environments, you'll be ready to link these calming moments to routine cues—like your morning coffee or your commute— making the practice automatic and always just a step away.

Make It Sticky: Turning 5-4-3-2-1 Grounding Into a Reliable Habit

Busy adults often find themselves using 5-4-3-2-1 grounding only in moments of crisis, grabbing the tool when anxiety or overwhelm spikes. While using grounding during tough moments can be calming, the next step is making it an automatic response—something your body starts before your mind even catches up. This does not depend on willpower alone; it's about weaving smart, simple supports into daily life. Moving grounding from 'good idea' to 'go-to habit' means setting up real-life hooks that prompt action without extra mental effort (Harvey et al., 2021).

Cue pairing is one of the most effective ways to lock in new habits by linking them to routines that already run on autopilot. Think about how you grab your seatbelt instinctively when sitting in a car or automatically check your phone first thing each morning. In the same way, you can anchor grounding exercises to daily events. For example, while waiting for coffee or tea to brew, spend thirty seconds doing a quick scan: spot five colors, touch four textures, listen for three sounds, notice two scents, and find one taste. Or, after typing your computer password, glance up and name three objects before diving into email. When crossing any doorway at home or work, reach out and notice two textures—the cool metal of the handle, the softness of your sleeve. Try these as easy 1-2-3 steps: pick your daily event, try the grounding sweep just once during the routine, and reflect for a few seconds if it felt natural or forced. Tweak timing or pairings until one sticks comfortably.

Tiny doses keep habits alive, even during the busiest weeks. The science shows that repeating a behavior in a stable context builds automaticity—your body starts linking the cue with the calming routine (Harvey et al., 2021). Rather than saving grounding for only big stresses, use micro-moments: set a quiet alarm labeled '60-second sense check' on your phone every hour, or piggyback on break times like elevator rides or Netflix loading screens. Even running through the first three steps of the exercise helps build consistency. It's better to do a short check-in many days than attempt longer, intense sessions rarely. Think of it like dental care: brushing twice daily protects more than a deep clean once a month.

Tracking wins is a powerful reinforcer. After a grounding sweep, rate your tension from 1–10 both before and after. Jot a brief note: 'Elevator—used touch, went from 7 to 5.' At week's end, review all entries. Highlight which cues worked best or which settings offered the quickest calm. Your brain is wired to remember what delivers results, so these notes strengthen the mental link between grounding and relief (Gaines, 2021). Plus, seeing even small improvements reminds you that progress comes in many forms. Each time you shave a point off your tension level, count it as a real win. This feedback keeps motivation steady long past the first try.

Visual reminders lighten the memory load during stressful moments and boost habit repetition. Stick a tiny colored dot on your laptop near the trackpad, your bathroom mirror, or even your wallet—where stress usually strikes. Next to the dot, add a cue word or phrase written on a sticky note: 'see blue, check senses,' or 'red = five things.' Move the dot if routines shift, like changing desks or switching daily patterns. These simple, flexible prompts act as environmental nudges, bringing grounding to mind right when you need it most. Dots can go on mirrors for busy parents hustling through morning routines, laptops for remote workers jumping between meetings, or inside wallets for those midnight spiralers reaching for comfort snacks.

Small setbacks are normal as new habits take hold. You may forget to ground yourself some mornings or skip a midday sense check altogether. That's perfectly fine—tiny, inconsistent steps count just as much as the perfect streak. Progress builds with practice, and starting matters more than perfection. Experiment until routines feel effortless. If one pairing doesn't fit, mix it up. Try different cues or time slots until something fits naturally into your day. Remember, building lasting habits isn't about flawless execution but about showing up, again and again, sometimes in small ways (Harvey et al., 2021; Gaines, 2021).

Pick one everyday event, a single sixty-second window, and one reminder—a colored dot, a gentle alarm, or a sticky note—you can set up today. By anchoring this practice now, you'll start turning 5-4-3-2-1 grounding into an automatic skill that stands ready when you need it. With these practical steps in place, the journey continues: soon, you'll explore how these habits help tackle deeper stress cycles and support emotional resilience throughout even the busiest seasons.

Final Thoughts

If thinking your way out of anxiety really worked, you'd have solved it by now. This chapter helped make sense of why battling thoughts in the heat of the moment often backfires. When anxiety spikes, debating with yourself only burns more mental fuel and leaves you feeling stuck. By shifting your focus to what's right here—what you can see, touch, hear, smell, and taste—you offer your body proof that you're safe. Grounding isn't about ignoring problems or pretending everything is fine; it's about giving your nervous system a break from constant alarms so you can get clarity and relief.

Remember, practicing grounding skills isn't about perfection or doing every step just right. It's about tiny choices in real situations—naming the color of your coffee cup, feeling your feet on the floor, noticing a faint sound. The more you use these moments to come back to your senses, the easier it gets for your brain to calm itself. Over time, this becomes less of a trick and more of a habit, something you reach for automatically when life ramps up. These small actions don't erase stress, but they do help you meet your days with steadier shoulders and a little more ease.

Chapter 4: Thought Parking Lot: Save It, Stop the Spiral

Have you ever tried to quiet your mind but found thoughts spinning faster instead? That endless loop of worries and to-dos isn't just tiring—it actually changes how your brain feels and works. When our minds get crowded with racing thoughts, it's like trying to juggle too many things at once; something has to slip or the whole act feels overwhelming. But there's a simple trick to break that spin: getting those thoughts out of your head. Writing them down or capturing them somewhere external doesn't just clear mental space—it shifts your brain's focus, easing tension and making room for clearer thinking.

This chapter invites you to explore why saving a thought outside your mind can stop the endless spiral of stress. You'll discover how offloading mental clutter changes your brain's experience and gives you power over those swirling ideas. Then, we'll walk through practical ways to catch and contain your thoughts so they don't keep buzzing inside, leaving you freer to tackle what really matters without the exhausting noise.

Why Externalizing Works

Think back to those moments when your mind felt packed with racing thoughts and nagging worries. That pressure builds, carving out space for tension, mistakes, and the feeling of being stuck. Earlier chapters helped you notice when your brain tips into overload. Now, there's relief in sight: externalizing thoughts—getting them out of your head and onto a page or screen—transforms that chaos into clarity.

Human working memory was never designed to juggle dozens of items at once. Picture a busy day: a grocery list rattles in one corner of your mind, project deadlines crowd another, and reminders to send an email pile on top. No matter how sharp or disciplined you are, brains can only hold a short list of details before dropping something important (Endres et al., 2011). That's why, when you try to carry everything at once, focus slips and stress grows. Think of your working memory like a phone with limited tabs—you open too many, it freezes. The act of jotting down tasks or worries closes those open loops and frees up mental space for what matters right now.

When you capture a runaway thought—like 'book dentist appointment' during a Zoom meeting—you turn off the background noise that drains energy. Researchers call this the Zeigarnik effect: unfinished business grabs your attention until your brain believes it's handled (Patwardhan et al., 2021). Writing something down sends a powerful signal to your mind, saying, 'It's safe. We have a record. You can move on.' This isn't just about ticking boxes; it's about easing nagging tension, shrinking anxiety, and letting go of constant self-reminders. For example, when you scribble 'pick up birthday gift' onto a sticky note instead of circling it mentally all afternoon, the urgency fades. Your brain trusts the list and lets you focus again.

Externalizing also gives you new perspective. Thoughts swirling inside your head often feel enormous and tangled, but once written down, they shrink to something concrete and workable. That sense of doom—"I'll never catch up"—turns into, 'Follow up with two emails, review slides, reschedule one meeting.' Seeing your thoughts from the outside takes away their power. It creates objectivity, so you can spot exaggerations and break tasks down. A busy parent staring at a whiteboard sees errands sorted and priorities clear, not a mess of unformed pressure. Written distance brings order to overwhelm, opening room for better decisions.

Lists don't only ease pressure; they hand back control. When everything lives in your head, choices blur together. By writing tasks or worries in a physical or digital 'Parking Lot,' you transform vague overwhelm into a menu of actions. You get the chance to decide: should I tackle, schedule, ask for help, or let this go? Decisions become clearer, and the constant cycle of remembering and forgetting finally quiets. Imagine scrolling through a simple list at the end of a busy day and feeling free to delete what's not urgent, slot a reminder where it belongs, or plan ahead without fear of missing something. Each item moves from a spiral of worry to an actionable next step, taking you out of reactive mode and putting you firmly back in charge.

Earlier, we saw how a crowded mind drives tension and mistakes. Here's what happens when you clear a little space: focus sharpens, emotion settles, and energy returns. Externalizing doesn't erase every problem, but it rewires the way you approach them. With this science in mind, you're ready to build a simple system that guards your focus and sanity every day. Now that you know why offloading matters, let's walk through a foolproof setup so every thought has a home.

The Parking Lot Setup

Now that you know why giving your mind a safe place to send spirals offers real relief, let's make sure you have a system that is ready whenever—and wherever—overthinking strikes. Sometimes, just understanding how writing down anxious thoughts helps is not enough in the rush of real life. What really matters is making it easy for busy, overloaded adults to capture thoughts before they take over. The following setup anchors the theory in daily routine and builds in self-kindness from step one.

Single Home Base

Most people already juggle sticky notes, apps, or loose scraps. Feeling scattered is normal. The first step is to pick ONE spot —a "home base" for every swirling thought. This single destination erases decision fatigue and prevents the stress of searching for ideas later. Start by looking at what you already use. If your phone is always in hand, consider using the "Notes" app or another simple notepad app. If you're more tactile, choose a small notebook or even index cards clipped together.

Next, decide where your home base will live: tucked by your computer, always in your bag, or as an icon pinned to your phone's main screen. Picture someone who defaults to their phone throughout the day—they might add the Notes app shortcut to their lock screen for instant access. Another example: someone at home places a bright notepad on the kitchen counter so it catches the eye while moving between tasks.

Make a gentle, no-pressure promise to yourself: move stray thoughts into this spot at least once per day. It does not need to be perfect. Even if you start with a single scribbled word, that counts as progress.

Quick Syntax

Many worry about capturing thoughts "the right way." Breathe easy—there are no rules for perfect notes. Under stress, short and direct works best. Use this quick template: action verb plus 3-5 word detail. It could look like "Call: clarify client need" or "Check: submit hours." To add context, try "Home," "Work," or "Health" so later you know where the thought belongs. For a work example: "Email: budget Q, Work." For home: "Buy: dog food, Home." A health note might be "Book: annual checkup, Health." The goal is to get it out of your mind fast, not to write full sentences. If the system feels messy, that's okay—it only needs to work for you.

Time Stamp

Writing the date helps prevent overwhelm later on. A little detail gives future-you context when reviewing the list. For each entry, jot today's date next to the thought. You might also add a quick urgency rating in parentheses—1 means low, 2 means soon, 3 means must-do. For example: "6/3: Email: travel refund (2)." If there's a deadline, add it too: "6/3: Pay rent (3)—due 6/5." This tiny step keeps things organized but never let it slow you down. Imperfect entries are better than none at all, so add details only when you can.

Review Ritual

You don't have to monitor your list all day. Give yourself two short check-ins: once around lunch and again as you wrap up work or before bedtime. Linking these reviews with other habits helps them stick—set an alarm, use the end of a meeting, or tie it to brushing your teeth. At each review, clarify notes that need more detail ("Email: budget Q" becomes "Email: budget Q for team trip?"), tag where thoughts belong, move anything urgent onto today's to-do, and leave low-urgency ideas parked for later. Not every thought needs action. Sometimes simply naming a worry and seeing it safely stored is enough. Imagine being stuck in traffic when a big vet bill pops into your head: just enter "Call: vet billing (2)." That thought waits until review time, so you can stay focused on the moment.

Adaptability is the strength of this practice. Whether you are running between meetings, juggling calls at the kitchen table, or winding down after a long day, a reliable parking lot keeps worries from circling endlessly. Even one parked entry is a victory for your nervous system. If setting up the whole system today feels tough, begin by parking a single thought. Progress counts at every stage. With your Parking Lot ready, you'll try it live using a brief, structured brain dump to unload loops fast.

Apply Now: 2-Minute Brain Dump

Now that your parking lot is set up—maybe it's a slim notebook or a notes app—you're ready for its first real test. This brain dump is the next step in moving worries from swirling around your mind into one safe, visible spot. If you've felt stuck with loops of to-dos or anxieties running in the background, this tool lets you pause, unload, and breathe. It's not about making order yet, just about clearing space so new things aren't always piling on top.

Unloading your mind can feel risky, like you might open a floodgate. Plenty of adults worry they'll make a mess or will see too much clutter on the page. That's okay. The mess is normal, and seeing it on paper is actually a sign the system is working (Allen, 2025; Nursing, 2025). You're moving from being trapped inside thought spirals to observing them— almost like stepping outside your own noisy house.

Settle into your everyday spot—a kitchen chair, car seat before an appointment, your office desk—and grab whatever you chose as your parking lot. No rules on place, posture, or gear. You can do this with a pen, a sticky note, your phone, even a kid's crayon if needed.

Set a timer for exactly two minutes. Any phone or old-school kitchen timer works. The short window isn't random—it helps your brain short-circuit perfectionism. Two minutes is fast enough that you won't get bogged down by feeling like everything must be explained or organized (Nursing, 2025). When the timer starts, start writing. Your job is to write down everything crowding your mind without any judgment or editing. Keep your pen or thumbs moving, even if what comes out is choppy, repetitive, or full of blanks.

Don't filter or tidy your thoughts. Write phrases, fragments, single words, or even draw squiggles if the words get stuck. Examples might include: "laundry on floor," "call boss back," "feel anxious about meeting," or even "ugh, I can't focus." There is no right format. Some people fill whole pages and others jot down six items. Both count. Remind yourself: the goal is unloading, not making sense yet (Allen, 2025).

You might hit patches where your inner critic pipes up. Maybe you wonder if this is silly, or get tempted to stop after thirty seconds. Keep going until the timer rings. If your hand stalls, just repeat the last word or scribble until another thought shows up. Momentum is better than completeness for now. Nobody will grade what appears here—this is your unfiltered map of today's mental traffic (Nursing, 2025).

Expect some entries to have zero obvious next step. Lots may sound jumbled or incomplete. That's fine. Your only task right now is capture. "Recorded is enough for now." If you worry midway about fixing or sorting, remind yourself that's next time's work. Relief often shows up as you list, not as you solve (Allen, 2025). Even when nothing looks neat or gentle on the page, you are giving your mind proof that you don't have to fix everything at once.

When the timer stops, set down your pen or device. Before moving away, scan your list. Notice if anything spikes a stronger feeling—jaw tightening, chest heaviness, an internal groan. Star or put an exclamation mark next to these. Maybe you see "get passport renewed" and suddenly your shoulders tense. Mark it. If several lines trigger you, quietly circle the one that feels loudest. These markings aren't for action yet— they're just gentle pointers for where your energy is most pulled right now.

As closure, take one slow inhale through your nose and then let out a long exhale through your mouth. Whisper, jot, or silently say—"It's saved. I'll review later." If saying this out loud feels awkward, type it into your app or just think it to yourself. After this, return to your previous activity for at least two minutes—answer an email, fold laundry, squeeze in some stretches—so your brain learns that dumping thoughts isn't a rabbit hole but a reset button (Allen, 2025; Nursing, 2025).

Any result is progress. Your page might hold disjointed lists, half-formed sentences, even blunt emotions. Every bit that lands on paper is a win. Whether you dumped five words or fifty, you paused the spiral and built evidence you can create relief on demand.

Soon, you'll learn to turn this list into clear choices—what to do, decide, delete, or delay—in the next section. For now, every captured item matters more than how neat it looks or how many you wrote. You're not just understanding the value of externalizing thoughts—you're practicing relief.

From Dump to Decision: Translating the Brain Dump Into Actionable Choices

After scribbling out all those swirling thoughts in your two-minute brain dump, you're probably looking at a jumble that feels honest but wild. Now everything is on paper, it's time to sort your list into concrete choices, so you don't get stuck in review limbo. This next move gives you more control and helps your mind breathe easier. Moving from chaos to clarity can feel like cleaning out an overflowing inbox—the difference is, you run the show. Here's how you turn a messy pile into something manageable.

Start by reading through your entire list without judging anything on it. It's normal to see odd or repetitive worries alongside practical tasks. Sorting takes only a few minutes but pays off with relief and a real sense of control. You'll be sorting each item into one of four buckets: Do, Decide, Delete, or Delay.

The "Do" Bucket: Quick Wins for Control

Think of this as your fast-track lane. Skim your list and highlight the one to three things you could finish in less than two minutes. These are small actions—pinging a colleague with a yes/no answer, confirming a calendar invite, or putting away a stack of mail. At home, maybe it's moving dirty tea mugs to the sink or texting your partner about dinner plans. For personal worries, maybe it's checking your bank balance or adding "call mom" to your phone reminders. Grab these wins now; when you cross them off right away, it's not just about shrinking your list. It gives your brain a quick dose of accomplishment, nudging overwhelm out of the way and making space for new energy.

- Step 1: Scan your brain dump for tiny tasks.
- Step 2: Star or circle up to three items you could finish almost instantly.
- Step 3: Do them right now if possible, then strike them off your Parking Lot list.
- Step 4: Pause to notice how even a little lightening of your load shifts your mood.

The "Decide" Bucket: Breaking Big Tasks Down

Some thoughts pop up because there's a decision hiding in them. These might look like "Finish quarterly project," "Plan summer vacation," or "Handle insurance paperwork." Anything too big or vague stays stuck. Take a moment to break these down into the smallest possible next step. "Email Jane for the project timeline," "Check flight dates for June," or "Call agent for policy details" make action possible.

Now pull out your phone, planner, or app and assign these steps a real time slot. You don't want a calendar filled with big goals—just one or two bite-sized moves per day. This keeps momentum strong while protecting you from overload.

- Step 1: Find large or open-ended tasks and rewrite them as tiny, clear actions.
- Step 2: Schedule these mini-actions into actual dates or time blocks.
- Step 3: Limit yourself to a handful (one to three) per day so you stay kind to future you.
- Step 4: Strike the rewritten version from your list after scheduling.

The "Delete" Bucket: Making Space With Permission to Let Go

Not every thought deserves permanent residence in your Parking Lot. Old reminders, outdated worries, or self-criticisms you can't act on (like "Why did I say that dumb thing last week?") all belong here. There are also notes and ideas that aren't pressing ("Book rec: 'Atomic Habits'"). If it doesn't serve today's priorities, cross it off with a satisfying line. If you want to save ideas for later, copy them to a separate "Archive" list—digital or in your journal. Practice saying to yourself, "This one's handled," "Not mine to fix now," or "Releasing this for today." Feel a gentle sense of closure as you mark these gone.

- Step 1: Find any worry, note, or nag lacking clear relevance or action.
- Step 2: Cross off right away if it's truly unnecessary.
- Step 3: Move non-urgent info or ideas to your Archive if you'd like.

- Step 4: Say your chosen release phrase out loud or quietly.

The "Delay Box": Deferring Without Stress or Avoidance

Certain thoughts aren't urgent but tend to stick around—like "Should I take that course?" or "Should I replace my old coat next year?" Let these rest in your "Delay Box." Create a spot on your Parking Lot page or a simple note on your phone. Label it clearly. Promise yourself you'll revisit these at your next review—maybe Friday afternoon. If an item is still unimportant after two weekly reviews, that's your cue to delete. This gentle structure means you aren't avoiding problems—you're showing yourself wise boundaries.

- Step 1: Identify any thought that isn't urgent, new, or actionable now.
- Step 2: List these in your designated Delay Box area.
- Step 3: Mark your next review date (sticky note, calendar event, app reminder).
- Step 4: After two reviews with no change, consider crossing out for good.

With your list sorted, pick one of your quick wins from the Do bucket and tackle it right away to cement your progress. Then set a reminder for your next Parking Lot review. With repetition, this routine grows trust in yourself—and proves that even the messiest mental spirals can be tamed, one gentle sort at a time.

Bringing It All Together

When your mind fills up and starts running in circles, it's easy to feel like there's no way out. Getting thoughts out of your head and into a safe spot—like a notebook or an app—can give you instant relief from overwhelm. This chapter showed how externalizing your thoughts not only eases mental pressure but also changes the way your brain responds to stress. It's not about being perfect or organized; it's about choosing a simple step that gives your busy mind room to breathe.

With these simple techniques, you can hit pause on spirals and regain clarity whenever you need it. Saving your thoughts means you don't have to keep remembering and re-remembering what matters—it lets you decide what needs your attention now, what can wait, and what you can let go of altogether. Each time you park a thought, you're building a system that supports focus and calm, not just for today but every day going forward.

Chapter 5: Leaves on a Stream: Unhook from Thoughts

Have you ever found yourself tangled up in thoughts that just won't quit, as if your mind is holding onto them tightly and won't let go? Instead of battling those thoughts head-on or trying to push them away, imagine what it would be like to simply step back and watch them float by without getting caught up. This isn't about winning a war against your mind but about shifting how you relate to your own thinking—a gentle unhooking rather than a fierce fight. It's the difference between deleting those unwelcome mental loops and gently loosening their grip through something called defusion.

This chapter invites you to explore this core shift in mindset: seeing your thoughts as passing experiences rather than commands to obey or problems to fix. By learning to observe your mind from a little distance, you begin to create space for calm and choice instead of struggle and overwhelm. Together, we'll build from recognizing the patterns that trap you to practical ways of stepping back, using imagery and language tweaks that help you loosen those thoughts' hold on you. It's about finding freedom not by silencing your inner chatter, but by changing your relationship with it in ways that fit naturally into your busy life.

Defusion, Not Deletion: Loosening the Grip of Unhelpful Thoughts

Spotting your mental spirals and labeling feelings has already laid the groundwork. You've learned to pause and name anxiety or overthinking as it shows up, almost like checking the instruments on a dashboard. Now that you can notice when you're stuck in a loop, what if you could ease up your grip on those thoughts—without needing to silence them? This section shifts the focus from control and fixing to freedom and flexibility. Instead of trying to delete worries, you'll learn to observe them from a slight distance.

Imagine your mind is a busy office, filled with notifications popping up all day. When a thought appears—'I'm not keeping up,' 'That meeting will go badly'—your old habit might be to dive right in, wrestle with it, or scramble to convince yourself otherwise. Defusion means stepping back and seeing each thought as just another pop-up, not a command or warning light. Picture using a dashboard view instead of climbing inside every alert. This move from being inside a thought to observing it lets you respond with more calm and choice—like noticing, 'There goes my over-preparing again,' and giving yourself one slow breath before acting.

Language is your most practical lever for this shift. Instead of saying, 'I'm anxious about this project,' try, 'I notice the thought that I might mess this up.' That tweak—adding 'I notice the thought'—breaks the spell of identification. The feeling may stay for a bit, but the urgency drops. Real-world example: Before sending an important work email, your mind says, 'They'll think this isn't good enough.' Rather than bracing for impact, say quietly, 'Noticing the thought: That wasn't good enough.' This small script works anywhere. During a tricky conversation with your kid, swap 'I'm failing as a parent' for 'That's the thought that I'm failing as a parent.' It puts a little daylight between you and the story running through your mind.

Here's the paradox: The more you struggle against unwanted thoughts, the more persistent they become. Trying to force out a worry only makes it louder, like telling yourself not to think about a catchy song stuck in your head. Consider those nights when you try to talk yourself out of a late-night fear, but end up going in circles. The harder you push against an anxious prediction or an old self-judgment, the tighter its grip. Defusion invites you to allow thoughts to exist—no persuading, arguing, or erasing. Instead, you let them float by, knowing you don't have to act on any of them.

This shift frees up mental space for action in line with your values. Your attention moves from endless debate to what actually matters in the next moment—maybe sending one honest reply, taking a brisk walk, or saying yes to a friend's call. When you stop spending all your resources on battling your mind, you gain energy for micro-actions that fit your true priorities. Each time you allow a worry to pass through without engaging in struggle, you reinforce a sense of agency. Even brief gaps between thought and reaction help build a new identity—one where your choices reflect who you want to be, not just what your mind shouts the loudest.

You're building on earlier skills: first noticing your inner loops, now learning to unhook without analyzing or fighting them. With these ideas in hand, you're ready for something more practical—a method you can use anywhere, not just in theory. Having set the mindset shift, the next step is a concrete practice that lets you experience defusion directly.

Leaves on a Stream: Guided Defusion Practice

Now that you've seen why being the witness matters, let's practice it together. This is where theory turns into something you can actually feel. The Leaves on a Stream image gives your mind a gentle nudge to step back from thoughts, noticing them without needing to debate or fight with them (Schenck, 2011; *Leaves on a Stream (Worksheet)*, n.d.). It's not about pushing thoughts away or doing it perfectly. It's more like settling in to watch clouds float by—sometimes they drift fast, sometimes slow, and sometimes you lose track for a moment. That's all part of learning a softer form of attention.

Begin by making yourself as comfortable as you can. Sit down wherever you are—on a chair, the floor, even at your desk if that's what works today. Plant your feet flat on the ground if possible, letting your hands rest in your lap or on your thighs. Feel the support underneath you. Let your eyes close, or just soften your gaze so the world becomes a little less sharp. Take a slow breath. Now picture yourself beside a stream—a real one you remember, or just invent a peaceful place in your mind. Imagine water moving gently, leaves floating on top, sunlight sparkling, maybe a cool breeze grazing your arms. If it's hard to see details clearly, that's fine. Some people hear the sound of water or just sense the feeling of calm. You can adapt this scene as needed. Eyes open is okay too if closing them feels uneasy (Schenck, 2011).

Set a timer for 3–5 minutes. Short windows keep this inviting instead of intimidating. Any length is enough to get started. Now, as you sit with the stream, notice whatever thought pops up. It could be 'I can't relax,' 'This is weird,' 'Laundry list tonight,' or just a memory or worry. Instead of following the thought or fighting it, put it on a leaf in your mind. Just name it softly—'Worried about work'—and place it on a leaf, letting it drift along the stream. There's no rush. If a leaf gets stuck on a rock or circles back, imagine it hanging out until it's ready to move. Each thought gets a leaf—even doubts like 'I'm not good at this.' Let those float too (Schenck, 2011; *Leaves on a Stream (Worksheet)*, n.d.).

Distraction is normal. At some point, your attention might chase after a thought, or you might realize you haven't pictured the stream for a while. That's okay. The trick here is kindness—notice, label it as 'Hooked,' and gently return to watching the next leaf. Treat each return as progress, not a setback. If your imagination runs dry or boredom hits, remind yourself there's no failing here. Even ten seconds of spacing out from a sticky thought can be a win. Some days, the exercise will feel clumsy or awkward; other times, you may settle in with a bit more ease. You can try this after a tough meeting in a parked car, while taking a break at your desk, or unwinding on the sofa. Make the scene yours—add favorite sounds, adjust the water speed, or just focus on grounding your feet as you breathe.

When your timer ends, take a steady breath. Gently come back to your space—wiggle your fingers, look around, maybe stand and stretch. Notice, even for a brief pause, if anything feels a little lighter. Even tiny moments where thoughts felt less sticky count. With regular practice, this skill starts to feel more natural, helping you trust that thoughts don't have to dictate your mood or actions (Schenck, 2011; *Leaves on a Stream (Worksheet)*, n.d.). Once you've tried this in a quiet moment, you can translate that ease into real-life, on-the-spot situations.

With the core experience in place, let's look at subtle language tweaks for quick relief.

Apply Now: Phrase Tweaks

Just a moment ago, you practiced letting thoughts float by with "Leaves on a Stream." That exercise shows how imagery can give you space from self-criticism or worry without fighting your mind. Still, in busy moments—standing in a grocery line, sitting through a tense meeting—you might not have the time or privacy to close your eyes. When life speeds up, phrase-based tweaks offer practical, right-now relief. With the imagery in place, quick verbal tweaks can deliver the same defusing effect in the middle of real life, giving you a way to loosen the hold of tough thoughts with nothing more than a shift in words.

One simple method is called "Name the Story." This may sound odd, but give it a try when your mind refuses to quiet down. Naming a familiar thought pattern as a story helps you see it's not a command, just an old mental script. When self-doubt pipes up after tough feedback at work, notice the loop and softly label it, "Ah, the 'not enough' story." No need to mock yourself or force detachment—just say it gently. If your mind keeps spinning before a deadline, pause and name it: "Here comes the 'I always mess up' story." This soft recognition changes the tone from fact to fiction. After naming your narrative, turn your attention to a chosen next step—answer an email, refill your water, or tidy up your desk. Agency returns in those seconds you claim back from the old script.

Try the "Sing the Thought" technique next time a perfectionist worry or fear of judgment loops in your mind. The idea is simple: change the sound, change its power. Choose a nursery rhyme or your favorite jingle, then sing the sticky phrase in your head or whisper it if you're alone. Even twenty seconds of singing "I'm never going to get this right" to the tune of "Happy Birthday" can seem ridiculous, but that's the point. When you feel silly or start to giggle, notice the awkwardness—this means the grip is loosening. Check in with yourself afterwards; does the thought feel lighter? If so, let it drift, or move on to your next activity.

Another tool is "Repeat Fast." When a self-critical thought won't quit—like after an argument or stressful family call—repeat the core phrase quickly and evenly for about twenty seconds. Out loud works best, but silent repetition is fine too. Focusing on speed turns the message into nonsense syllables: "not good enough, not good enough, not good enough..." until your brain hears sound instead of meaning. Stop, take a slow breath, and check if there's even a margin of relief or distance from the feeling caught in that loop. You don't have to erase the thought, only feel some slack appear so you can return to what matters around you.

For a gentler approach, "Thank the Mind" offers a reset without struggle. Invite yourself to say, either silently or aloud, "Thanks, mind, for trying to help," when anxious planning or blame repeats. Recognizing your brain's intent—even when bothersome—lowers resistance and self-blame. End by choosing a purposeful action, however small: send one message, close a browser tab, or get a glass of water. This nod to your mind's effort keeps you engaged in life instead of locked in argument with every thought.

These micro-practices fit anywhere—at your desk, on a walk, during conversation. Try them out first in easy situations, like a mild Monday morning guilt loop or late-night rumination over something small, when pressure is low. There's no single right way to use these tools. Experiment, mix, match, and notice even the smallest progress. On some days, you'll find these phrase tweaks peel off distress like tape. Other times, they might barely budge strong feelings—and that's normal too. For those high-emotion days, the next section will guide you to fallback supports when phase tweaks aren't quite enough. Each skill builds toward flexibility, not perfection, so permission to start small and keep returning as needed.

When Defusion Feels Flat: Troubleshooting Real-World Stuck Moments

Sometimes, even though you've tried the leaf-on-a-stream image or changed your defusion phrase three times, anxiety still clings tight. Your mind replays that meeting misstep or tomorrow's deadline, heart pounding as if nothing is helping. If you recognize this, you're in good company—this is part of learning, not a sign you're stuck forever. When classic defusion feels flat, it's time to gently switch gears and try some practical resets. Small pivots can make a surprising difference, especially on busy, loaded days.

Body First: Grounding Before Thinking

When tension is high, the body can hijack mental skills. In those moments, calming the nervous system helps every other tool work better. One simple way is the 4-6 breath: inhale through your nose for four counts, let the air fill your belly, pause, then exhale slowly through pursed lips for six counts. Repeat this four times. If thoughts are stormy during a tense meeting or after sharp feedback, press both feet firmly into the floor, tune into their solidness, and let your toes and heels relax. You can also look around and quietly name five things you see—the corner of your laptop, the blue pen, a window, your coffee mug, your shoes. These tiny resets soothe jitters enough to make space for thought-based techniques again (Nash, 2022). Notice if there's even a tiny drop in your chest or one deeper breath; that's your progress. If physical discomfort remains, stay with the breath—sometimes you need a few more rounds before trying another step.

One Thought Only: Narrowing the Focus

Drowning in a swirl of worries? Trying to manage every anxious loop at once is like shushing a whole dinner party. Instead, pick out the loudest "guest"—the thought that wakes you up at 3am, or the one stealing your attention at work. Write this thought on a sticky note or type it out. Treat it as just words, imagining it floating by on its own little leaf. Give yourself permission to let the rest wait; you're picking the biggest block for now (*Cognitive Defusion Techniques and Exercises*, 2022). Sometimes easing up on just this one thought creates space around everything else too. Progress might feel like a single loop slowing down or your shoulders dropping half an inch. If overwhelm returns, refocus on the most present worry—even if it's different each time you pause.

Short Bursts: Practice in Sips, Not Sprints

Long, perfect practice isn't required. Real progress with defusion comes from casual, quick tries scattered through busy hours. Pick three ordinary cues in your day—a kettle about to boil, elevator doors closing, an app updating—to do sixty seconds of watching thoughts float or saying "I'm noticing a worry about the project launch." Let this be casual. Five small tries beat one marathon session. For example, a parent waiting in the school pickup line can close their eyes for a moment, notice the inner chatter, and picture each thought drifting by without judgment. Micro-practices let you stay engaged with life rather than fighting for perfect calm. You'll know it's working if you catch yourself remembering to practice at all, or feeling present for just one minute. If you forget or your mind rebels, no problem—just start fresh with the next cue.

Values Cue: Tying Action to What Matters

Getting unhooked from sticky thoughts is easier when you follow defusion with a small act that lines up with what matters most to you. After you've practiced watching a worry float, do something tiny yet meaningful—reply to the message from your teammate, refill your water, tell your child "good job" after a tough day. These steps redirect focus onto values instead of anxiety's demands (Nash, 2022). For a high-achiever, that might mean sending a quick encouragement to a colleague instead of ruminating about feedback. If social pressure is building, text someone you trust right after defusing, even with a simple emoji. Track these micro-wins in a notebook or note app; each check mark shows momentum, even if your mind says otherwise. When motivation sags, reading past micro-wins can remind you how often you've responded, not just reacted.

Gentle Tweaks and Mindful Pauses

Some days, nothing seems to land. That's okay. On such days, try stacking two methods—maybe grounding first, then narrowing to one thought. Or double up on short bursts when meetings pile up. Adjust timing, mix methods, or invent your own imagery. There's no pass-fail here—just experiment until you find a bit of ease. The real measure of progress isn't a silent mind but a willingness to reset again and again. Each attempt brings you closer to living from your own values rather than someone else's script. With these troubleshooting strategies, keep pairing defusion with value-driven actions as you finish this chapter. These small shifts lay a real path away from spirals and toward momentum, one micro-win at a time.

Final Thoughts

Letting go of the need to control your thoughts is a new way forward—one that relieves some of the pressure you've been carrying. This chapter has offered a shift: instead of fighting with every worry or trying to force negative self-talk to disappear, you can step back and see each thought for what it is—just a passing mental event. Defusion gives you space between what pops up in your mind and how you choose to respond. By practicing gentle methods like letting thoughts float away, using quick language tweaks, and remembering that it's okay not to get it perfect, you start to loosen the grip those patterns have on your day-to-day life.

The key idea here isn't about erasing or silencing your mind—it's about freedom, flexibility, and reclaiming your own energy for things that matter most to you. Even if some thoughts stick around, you now have practical tools to meet them differently. Every time you notice and unhook from an old story, you build confidence in your ability to move forward with more ease and intention. Remember, progress comes in small steps, and even a little extra breathing room from overthinking is worth celebrating. By keeping these strategies close, you'll find yourself better equipped to ride out the busier moments and stay connected to what truly matters.

Chapter 6: Micro-Dose Muscle Release: Ease Tension, Clear Head

Did you know that within just half an hour of concentrating at work, more than 70% of adults start clenching their jaw or hunching their shoulders? Researchers who used sensors in offices found this common physical response to focused tasks. Even better, brief muscle-release exercises lasting only about a minute can lower the tension people feel by nearly a third on that very same day. This isn't about hitting the gym; it's about tiny doses of relief right when your body needs it most. These small actions offer a powerful way to ease built-up tightness before it snowballs into bigger stress.

This chapter dives into how these quick muscle releases break the cycle where tension fuels anxious thinking and keeps your brain stuck in high alert. You'll discover why tight muscles trick your mind into thinking danger is near, and learn simple, fast techniques to soften that grip. By understanding and interrupting this feedback loop, you can clear mental clutter and find calm without disrupting your busy day. Let's explore how these little moments of motion can create big shifts in how you feel and think.

Tension–Thought Feedback Loop

You've already seen how thoughts can spiral and stress responses fire when life gets overwhelming. Maybe you've traced your own pattern of ruminating about work late into the night, or noticed how one anxious thought breeds another until you're stuck in a loop you can't shake. But what happens when your body is the one pressing the panic button? Muscle tension isn't just a side effect—it's often fueling the mental noise that keeps you on edge.

Muscle tightness sends noisy signals up to your brain—a kind of bottom-up static that amplifies worry, frustration, and restless looping. Your shoulders might tense up after an email lands the wrong way; your jaw might clench without you even noticing at a long stoplight or before a difficult meeting. It's like wearing a suit of armor that's outgrown you—heavy, stiff, and impossible to ignore. The brain reads these physical cues as evidence that something's not right. Instead of calming down, it goes on high alert, scanning for threats and spinning stories to explain why you feel so uneasy. This feedback loop means that tension can kickstart anxious thinking, which tightens your muscles further, locking you into a cycle of stress (Chu et al., 2024). For many high-achieving adults, the pattern shows up most after hours spent frozen over a keyboard, stuck in traffic, or multitasking through demanding calls. Body tension is not just background noise—it's a blaring siren pulling your focus back to discomfort again and again.

Some areas send the loudest signals. The jaw, neck, and brow act as a trio of stress broadcasters. Clenching your teeth anchors worry in your face and head, making it harder to relax even during downtime. A stiff neck from too much screen time or bracing before tough feedback limits both range of movement and mood. The brow furrows during concentration or irritation, sending subtle cues to yourself (and everyone else) that you're on guard. These three sites work together, wiring your body's startle reflex and vigilance pattern straight into everyday work routines. Notice the locked jaw before a big video call or the ache in your temples after troubleshooting a crisis at work—these signs matter. When these muscles stay tense, they trick your brain into thinking danger is always just around the corner. Quick check-in: unclench your jaw for ten seconds and notice any shift that follows. Even a small release can dial down the alarm system and help your mind find a bit more space.

When tension hangs around these upper-body hotspots, it messes with your breath. Muscles tighten, restricting airflow and shifting breathing into the upper chest, where each inhale feels shallow and unsatisfying. The nervous system loses access to its natural brakes—the vagal pathways that slow your heart rate and signal safety—because those brakes depend on free, easy diaphragm movement (American Psychological Association, 2024; Chu et al., 2024). If your shoulders are up near your ears, try exhaling as fully as possible. You might notice a little more ease, a tiny drop in heart rate, or simply a fuller breath following the release. This chain reaction shows why muscle relaxation matters for stress —you can't talk your way out of fight-or-flight if your body believes you're still facing trouble.

Physical tension acts like extra browser tabs running in the background of your brain. Every twinge, throb, or ache waves a flag for your attention, draining energy away from clear thinking and flexible problem-solving. Your body's discomfort crowds your mental desktop, narrowing your field of focus and making routine tasks feel harder than they are. Once you learn to spot and release tension quickly, you reclaim that precious mental bandwidth. You'll find it easier to make decisions, bounce back from frustrating moments, and even enjoy brief windows of calm between the day's demands. Now that you know how tension fuels the noise, let's give you a simple, 60-second tool to break the loop right at your desk.

60-Second Release Circuit

This circuit is your fast track to releasing built-up tension and reclaiming mental clarity—without needing a full workout or special equipment. Many readers in this book are high-achieving adults managing busy schedules, working in challenging environments, and often feeling the weight of emotional and physical stress. Each step in this sequence is chosen to interrupt the muscle-thought feedback loop described earlier: as you soften key muscles, your brain can downshift from vigilance into a calmer, more capable mode. No gym clothes needed—just a willingness to give your muscles sixty seconds of focused attention.

Jaw Unclench

Target areas: Jaw, temples, ear area
Difficulty: Beginner
Duration: 45 seconds (plus a brief reset)
Steps:

1. Sit or stand upright with shoulders relaxed.
2. Place the whole tongue gently on the roof of your mouth, just behind your front teeth.
3. Press tongue upwards against the palate firmly—but without strain—for 5 seconds. Breathe normally.
4. Release tongue, letting your jaw hang slightly open (lips closed or parted), and relax for 10 seconds. Focus on warmth and slackness spreading through the jaw and around your ears.
5. Repeat steps 3–4 three times total.
6. After the final round, swallow once slowly to reset. Notice if tension near your temples or ears has reduced.

Modification: If pressing the tongue feels difficult, try the move with less pressure and shorter holds; increase as able. If you have jaw pain or TMJ disorder, never push through sharp pain. Always stop if discomfort rises. For extra support, add gentle jaw opening/closing while keeping the tongue up, following advice from clinical resources (*TMJ Exercises for Pain Relief | Colgate®*, n.d.; *Neck and Jaw Stretching Exercise - University of Mississippi Medical Center, 2024*).

Shoulder Squeeze

Target areas: Shoulders, upper back, neck
Difficulty: Beginner
Duration: 12–18 seconds
Steps:

1. Sit or stand tall, arms at your sides.
2. Inhale and lift both shoulders toward your ears, squeezing gently but comfortably for 3 seconds.
3. On a slow exhale, drop your shoulders heavily down. Immediately add a gentle shake for 2–3 seconds—like wiggling off static.
4. Repeat this inhale–squeeze, exhale–drop–and shake sequence two times total.

Common mistakes: Don't hunch forward or tense your neck—keep your spine long and breathe smoothly. Focus the movement in the shoulders, not by tensing your neck or jaw. If shoulder mobility is limited, reduce range and time.

Hand Reset

Target areas: Hands, forearms, palms, fingers
Difficulty: Beginner
Duration: About 25 seconds per side
Steps:

1. Clench both fists tightly for 5 seconds, noticing the forearms activate.
2. Open hands wide—spread fingers away from palms—and hold at full stretch for 5–8 seconds.

3. Use the thumb of one hand to press and slowly circle the center of the opposite palm for 10–15 seconds. Apply only comfortable pressure—no pain.
4. Switch hands and repeat.
5. Finish by gently stretching fingers back (one at a time or together) and shaking both hands loosely for 2 seconds.

Body awareness tip: If grip strength or mobility is limited, reduce squeeze time or pressure. Keep wrists straight and avoid overextending fingers. The palm massage softens hidden tension that builds up while typing or gripping devices all day.

Brow Smooth

Target areas: Brow, forehead, around eyes
Difficulty: Beginner
Duration: 10 seconds
Steps:
1. Lightly place index and middle fingers at the bridge of your nose, right above where glasses rest.
2. Glide fingertips along each eyebrow outward toward the temples using light-to-moderate pressure, keeping the forehead smooth and eyes soft.
3. Exhale fully as you reach your temples; pause briefly.
4. Repeat this tracing motion twice.
5. Notice if any frown lines ease and if your visual field feels wider or brighter.

Modifications: If skin is sensitive, lower the pressure or use only one finger per brow. Try the motion with eyes closed to increase relaxation.

Each move flows smoothly into the next—jaw then shoulders, then hands, then brow—to mimic the progression of tension release that best supports focus recovery throughout your day. This sequence is designed for practicality—you can do it seated or standing, and no one needs to know you're sneaking in micro-relief between meetings or calls. Any discomfort should always stay in the mild stretch zone, and breathing should remain relaxed throughout.

Next, we'll show you how to run a stealth version of this release circuit anywhere—including your desk or public spaces —so you're always equipped with tension-busting tools no matter where you are.

Apply Now: Desk-Friendly Version

Think back to the last time you practiced a 60-second muscle release circuit in a private spot. Many people find those moves effective, but tension climbs even faster when you're stuck at your desk, in a meeting, or working through emails—places where basic stretches feel awkward. This is where invisible micro-resets come in. You don't have to choose between ignoring the tension or waiting for a break room. Every small move brings relief, helping interrupt the cycle of tight muscles and racing thoughts.

Tiny resets work best when they fit into what you're already doing. Picture this: you're in the middle of a Zoom call, feeling the burn in your shoulders, or reading another tense message about deadlines. These moments are ripe for a stealthy micro-release. Each practice below steps you through a simple, desk-friendly reset. Try one now—even just reading it counts as progress. Check in with yourself before and after by rating your tension or breath ease from 0 to 10. Dropping even one point deserves credit.

Micro-Squeeze Release: Feet and Hands

- Press both feet flat on the floor.
- Squeeze the toes inside your shoes for three counts.
- Let go, then press your heels down for another count of three.
- Rest. Notice if the legs feel less buzzy.
- Gently wrap your fingers around your coffee mug, water bottle, or a soft scarf for twenty seconds. If that's not available, roll a pen between your hands.
- Unclench, shake out gently under your desk, and thank your hands for working so hard. These little reps tell your nervous system it's safe to reset (the Healthline Editorial Team, 2017).

Jaw and Shoulder Reset: Invisible Softening

- Sit tall, shoulders loose. Pretend to chew slowly without opening the mouth.
- Next, raise both shoulders up toward your ears. Hold for five seconds, then drop them. Repeat two times.

- Breathe and let your arms relax at your sides or on the armrests.
- Optional: If jaw pain flares, stop and relax your face; skip the jaw movement if sensitive (Le, 2025).
- Notice any warmth or softness around your neck and upper back? Give yourself credit for checking in.

Glute and Lower Back Tension Breaker

- Clench your glutes as if holding a coin. Count to five. Let go.
- Scoot to the edge of your chair, plant both feet firmly. Picture a gentle string pulling the crown of the head up, lengthening the spine without arching the back.
- Drop your ribcage slightly and notice space appear along your lower back and waistline.
- Let your breath fill the belly, then exhale slow.
- If sitting long, lift one knee toward the chest under your desk for a few seconds, switch sides. All these moves can happen while replying to emails or listening during a call (the Healthline Editorial Team, 2017; Le, 2025).

Prop Assist: Built-In Tools for Soothing

- Warm ceramic mug? Wrap both palms around it and breathe for a count of ten. Feel the heat soften palm and forearm tension.
- No mug? Try hugging a cushion or pressing palms together in your lap like prayer hands for fifteen seconds.

- Let your wrists rest soft against the desk edge instead of flexed upward. Feel your face relax as hand muscles let go (Le, 2025).

Timer Cue: Automatic Habit Helper

Phones, smartwatches, or even calendar reminders make it easier to remember micro-moves. Set a subtle vibration, or use calls and emails as cues. Rate jaw tension, brow tightness, or breathing smoothness before and after each mini-exercise. If numbers nudge lower, mark it mentally as a win. Missed a cue? Just jump in on the next round—a streak starts with one rep. Over time, these tiny resets build a strong stress-busting habit (the Healthline Editorial Team, 2017).

Posture Ping: Reset and Adjust

When slumping sneaks in, do a quick reset:
- Scoot forward, feet flat.
- Stack your ears, shoulders, and hips in a straight line. Imagine a light cord running from tailbone to top of head.
- Angle your laptop higher by stacking books underneath, easing neck and brow strain.
- Roll shoulders back gently, relax your jaw.
- Smile softly and celebrate a job well done, no matter how brief the effort.

Every body is different, and every day brings new tension patterns. If you ever feel pain, pause and adjust. One step or one squeeze is still progress. If you notice discomfort with certain moves, try the gentlest version, swap in another trick, or simply shift your breath. Soon, we'll cover easy tweaks for bodies that are sensitive, injured, or need extra care—helping you find comfort and calm through every season of stress.

Customize for Sensitive Bodies

You've just followed the hands-on, desk-friendly release guide. For some, these drills slide into the day without a hitch. For others—living with sensitive joints, pain, or hypermobility—a move or stretch that works for one body can feel wrong or set off a spiral of discomfort. Body-based skills should work for everyone, with the right adjustments. If your body is sensitive, in pain, or hypermobile, a few tweaks keep all the benefits while staying comfortable—here's how.

Range Respect

Pain, injury, and hypermobility demand a different approach. Instead of aiming for the full stretch or pushing to the edge, the goal is 40–60% effort. This zone minimizes flare-ups and overuse. Try this as your rule: "If it feels pokey, sharp, or escalating, skip it or soften it—no exceptions." Muscle release should carry mild "stretchiness," not strain. Shorten hold times or add rests instead of repeating sets back-to-back. For moves asking for large ranges, swap to small, slow contractions or simply tense and relax the muscle without changing joint angle. If you live with Ehlers-Danlos syndrome or similar conditions, make control your anchor—stay in the motion that feels steady, pause if you notice a shake, and never force a stretch past comfort.

If discomfort pops up:
- Return to your home position (neutral)
- Scan: Is this pain sharp, new, or spreading? If yes, stop the session
- Check for swelling, redness, or tingling—if it appears, take a longer break
- Use "less not more" as your default

Breath Pairing

Pairing release drills with breath amplifies relaxation and restores balance. A longer exhale tells the nervous system all is safe, lowering tension. Try cues like "inhale for two, exhale for six," or softly whispering "haaa" on the out-breath, like letting steam escape—not a forced sigh. If you feel lightheaded: reduce the depth of breath, slow your pace, and pause between reps. This isn't just about taking deeper breaths; it's about using timing and intention so release becomes automatic—a built-in reset switch. Science shows that slow, conscious exhalation can settle stress chemicals and ease overall pain levels (NHS, 2023; Geneen et al., 2017).

Support Tools

Let your props do half the work. Environmental support boosts comfort and makes release rituals more predictable, especially if fatigue or pain flares suddenly. Keep a neck pillow at your chair for easy posture shifts or wedge a rolled towel behind your lower back. Heat packs loosen tight muscles before drills—apply warmth (not hot) for ten minutes to soothe and prep. Use a tennis or massage ball for gentle foot or hand release, rolling without pressure over bony spots. Try propping your arms with cushions or placing a soft scarf under sensitive joints. Real office life trick: stash a small pillow at your workstation as a cue to take micro-breaks, or keep a ball under your desk to roll your feet while answering emails. Always use props before moving into any tension-release— never as a fix afterwards when soreness sets in. Each aid becomes a step in making daily release something you look forward to rather than a hassle or risk.

Medical Caution

Staying safe is part of self-care. Red flags mean stop immediately: chest pain, new or spreading numbness, persistent tingling, severe headache, or anything that feels "different" or worrisome. If you're healing from injury or have connective tissue challenges, always check with your clinician before starting new drills. Checking in isn't weakness, it's wisdom—these tools should serve you, not risk you. Make a quick safety check routine: "Do I feel my usual self? Is anything new happening? Is there any swelling or sharp pain?" If yes to any, pause and reach out for advice before going further. Never let self-management become self-pressure.

Every modification is a tool, not a limitation—it's how these body skills become truly yours. Picking what fits your needs makes micro-dosed release a real act of agency, not just another item on your task list. Let's close this session by choosing one micro-release you'll use as your default reset and setting a cue for it today. Set a phone alert or pair it with a routine action, like sipping your morning coffee or opening your laptop. This habit forms the backbone for progress in upcoming chapters—personalizing every step while proving that comfort and results can grow side by side.

Bringing It All Together

Over the last few pages, we've seen just how quickly tension can build in the body as you dive into focused work. Whether it's jaw clenching, shoulder hunching, or that creeping tightness in your brow, these muscle habits aren't just background noise—they send nonstop signals to your brain that keep you feeling alert, restless, and often more stressed than you realize. The big takeaway here? You don't need an hour at the gym or a full meditation session to break this tension loop. Simple, bite-sized release drills—just a minute at your desk or during daily routines—can make real changes in how much pressure you carry, both physically and mentally.

Small steps add up fast. When you use these quick resets throughout your day, you're sending your mind and body the message that it's okay to pause, breathe, and let go—even if only for sixty seconds. Over time, these micro-moves help clear mental static, restore focus, and give you back some calm in the middle of your busiest moments. Remember, every little release counts. Find what feels good and try it whenever stress creeps in; your muscles (and your mind) will thank you.

Chapter 7: If–Then Plans: Pre-Choose Calm Under Pressure

Imagine two coworkers sitting side by side when their phones buzz with a late work message from their boss at 4:57 p.m. One immediately freezes, heart racing and mind flooding with worries: "Did I miss something important?" By the time they leave work, that anxious energy clings tightly—muscles tense, thoughts swirling nonstop—and it follows them through their commute, creeping into their evening and stealing sleep. Meanwhile, the other coworker experiences that same jolt but reacts differently. Spotting the rush of tension, they take a slow breath in for four counts, hold it steady for four, then let it out gently for another four, repeating this just twice. Ten minutes later, the knot of stress loosens, and their night stays peaceful. This isn't about who's tougher or more laid-back; it all comes down to having a plan ready before the heat hits.

What made the difference? It wasn't luck or personality but a pre-decided if–then plan—a simple mental formula linking a stressful trigger to a calming action. In the moments when anxiety starts to climb, these tiny, precise plans give you a clear path forward, cutting through the fog of overwhelm. Instead of hoping to "stay calm," which often slips away under pressure, you train your brain to spot the cue and automatically follow through on a soothing step. This chapter dives into why crafting these specific if–then connections works so much better than vague good intentions, showing how you can transform sudden stress into signals for calm, all by planning ahead.

Implementation Intentions 101: The Science of Pre-Choosing Calm

Spotting a stress spiral before it takes over is a real achievement. Recognizing that tight chest or the buzzing phone just as your thoughts start to race means you're already doing what many never do: catching the moment before it runs away with you. Still, being able to notice a cue doesn't always make calm follow. So many ambitious adults set mental reminders to 'keep cool' only to watch calmness slip away in the next pressure spike. In stressful moments, generic hopes like "I'll stay calm" tend to vanish because the brain struggles to make clear decisions when pressure hits.

This is where the idea of an if–then plan changes everything. Picture this: instead of saying, "I'll handle stress better," you anchor your response to an exact trigger. 'If my inbox pings at 4:45 pm and my heart skips, then I will stand up and stretch my shoulders.' This cue–action link works because the plan lives right alongside your stress signal, turning what used to be a vague impulse into a direct instruction. Suddenly, there's no question about what to do; the moment the cue appears, so does your action. You aren't searching for the willpower to respond—you follow a path already mapped out for chaos.

Behavioral research shows that these plans connect the recognition of a stressor directly to the micro-action you want, creating a shortcut through old habits (Wieber et al., 2015).

Building on your growing awareness of early warning signs, it helps to know why making these links ahead of time matters so much. Stress hijacks decision-making just when you need clarity most. Imagine your mind as a browser with only a few tabs open—during a pressure spike, all but one or two tabs freeze. Trying to think up solutions while frazzled is like adding new tabs to a glitchy computer. Many report blanking out on skills they've practiced, simply because their brains feel overloaded. This is called decision fatigue. If–then plans work like having a sticky note taped to your desktop: the choice is made when you still have mental room, not when your system is maxed out. Studies show this "decision relief" lets you act without extra analysis, saving your energy for what comes next (Wieber et al., 2015).

These pre-set cue–action connections don't just help the first few times—they get easier with use. Every time you run your if–then plan, that pathway in the brain lights up more quickly. Think about how a well-worn path through grass becomes clearer each time it's traveled. On those tough days when willpower is gone and fatigue is high, this automatic route takes over. Instead of asking yourself, "How should I react?" you step straight into the behavior you've rehearsed. Research in habit formation finds that mental links between cues and actions can fire so quickly they outpace conscious deliberation, putting new routines on autopilot—even when your mind is tired or distracted (Wieber et al., 2015). That's a main reason these plans outperform broad advice or motivational pep talks under pressure.

The last piece of the puzzle is context. A strong if–then plan is never just about "being calm." It needs to match real-life details: time, location, sensation. For one busy adult, a useful plan might be: 'If my stomach flips as I walk toward the afternoon team call, then I turn off notifications and breathe slowly for four counts.' Another could look like: 'If my jaw tenses after hearing the same feedback again, then I press my feet into the floor and count down from five.' Generic cues ("if I'm stressed") miss the mark because they don't ground you in the specifics of your world. The more personal and sensory the cue, the more reliably your brain pulls up the right action. Women juggling home deadlines or late-night emails might create tailored anchors for those moments, linking feelings or surroundings (the hum of the dishwasher, the pause before opening Zoom) to soothing responses. Real-world context turns a written plan into a practical tool that fits your life's actual rhythms (Wieber et al., 2015).

With the why in place, the next step is making it practical— let's build three core if–then plans tailored to your top triggers.

Build Three Core Plans

You've already mapped your stress cues and named the moments that hijack your focus. Up until now, you've explored why pre-chosen actions work where willpower falters, and how connecting a stress cue to a small, do-able step can short-circuit the spiral. This is where flash insight becomes real-world strategy. By building three personal if–then plans, you take the groundwork of awareness and turn it into action when pressure hits—not after things calm down, but exactly when you need it most.

Start with Trigger Pick. Look back over your last two weeks for those points where tension spiked or thoughts spun out. Scan emails, calendar reminders, or simply replay a typical day in your mind. Watch for "early" warning signs: clenched jaws in meetings, shallow breaths before checking texts, or that restless feeling right as bedtime approaches. Mark the triggers that stand out—maybe they show up again and again, or maybe just once but throw you completely. Examples might include: an unexpected reschedule from your boss, a late-night memory loop about a tough conversation, or seeing a financial reminder pop up on your phone. Circle three. Your picks don't need to be dramatic; even small, annoying stumbles can snowball if left unchecked. Prioritize by frequency—the ones that keep returning—or pick based on which leave you more rattled. Trust your gut; you know when something trips you up.

With your triggers chosen, start Action Match for each. You want something brief, portable, and realistic. This isn't the time for hour-long practices or disappearing acts. Think 60–120 seconds. Ask, "Where am I when this comes up? What can I actually do there?" For a calendar crisis, box breathing at your desk works. In a group setting, pressing your palms together under the table resets your body without anyone knowing. If bedtime rumination is your stuck point, a quick sensory scan works right in bed. If you aren't sure what fits, try these ideas:

- Two rounds of box breathing (inhale four counts, hold, exhale four counts, hold)
- The 5-4-3-2-1 sensory grounding (see five things, touch four, listen for three, smell two, taste one) (Smith, 2018)
- Progressive muscle relaxation (clench/release fists and jaw)
- Silently repeating a calming phrase out of sight
- A slow bathroom break for a minute away

Pick one action per trigger. Choose what feels practical—even if it's tiny. If you doubt a choice will help, go for the smallest step. Discreetness counts: pressing fingertips together, slowing your breath, or privately tensing/releasing muscles are all fair game. Give yourself permission to make it barely noticeable. Any step keeps the loop from growing.

Next, nail down Exact Wording. The classic structure is: "If [trigger], then I [action]." The more clear and actionable the statement, the better. Skip wishy-washy verbs like "try," "hope," or "aim." Go straight for concrete moves: "do," "breathe," "count," "scan." Here are a few ready-to-use samples:

- "If my phone vibrates with a late email after 7pm, then I set it face-down and take two deep breaths before opening."
- "If a calendar change notification makes my shoulders tense, then I roll my shoulders back and count to eight while exhaling."
- "If I catch myself rerunning an old meeting after dark, then I look around my room and name five objects until I feel present again."

  Notice how each plan describes the visible sign (shoulders tense, phone buzz, mind racing) and matches it to an exact, short reset. Write your three if–then plans out, word for word. Speak them aloud. Listen for any confusing or vague steps—clarity matters here. Lone intentions get lost when adrenaline surges; crisp instructions stay findable.

Set your plans in motion with Practice Reps. Don't wait for real stress to crash in. Each morning, read your three statements out loud, picturing the situation as clearly as possible. Repeat in the evening before bed. At least once in your day, run through one if–then plan—either during a real-life moment or in a low-stakes setting. Put a tally mark, check box, or smiley face next to each rep. There's no test and no score at stake— just training your brain and body to spot the cue and run the move. Doing reps will feel odd at first. Many give up after a day, thinking awkward means bad. Treat every attempt as proof you're wiring in a new option. None of this asks for perfect delivery. Showing up for reps teaches your mind new routes, so you're not scrambling the next time stress hits unexpectedly.

You may notice some discomfort as you put these plans into motion—maybe even a dash of self-doubt or awkward laughter. That's not failure; it's proof you're nudging at old patterns and letting new ones form. These experiments aren't pass/fail. Try, tweak, celebrate small wins, and rewrite any plan that feels clunky. You're making change possible in moments that used to feel impossible. With your plans written and rehearsed, it's time to field-test them during real stress and refine quickly.

Apply Now: Plan in the Wild

You've chosen your top three if–then plans, written them out, and rehearsed how they'll look whenever a stress trigger pops up. Until this point, everything has happened on paper or in a safe practice run—now comes the part that turns these intentions into lived skill. This is where you take your personal plans into the real world and let real events shape your tools. Practice here transforms planning into steady action. Each test run, no matter the outcome, rewires your responses so your body and mind start working together under pressure.

Real mastery blooms only when you meet actual stress with your prepared actions. Imagine your work inbox pings at 8:59 a.m.—your heart skips or your jaw tightens. Or, you get a family group text that sets off the first flash of irritation. These are perfect moments to deploy your pre-chosen calm. Spot that physical cue—the first twinge of heat, sinking stomach, clenched jaw—then launch your if–then plan within five seconds. Give yourself 60–120 seconds to run the action, whatever it may be: slow exhale, pressing feet into the floor, a sensation check. Afterward, pause and check what your body feels. Relaxation in your shoulders? Heartbeat returning to steady? If you stumbled, that's part of the experiment—the most learning comes from noticing what tripped you up.

Real life brings surprise and mess. For some, this means using an if–then plan when Slack chat blows up right before a deadline; for others, it's calming their breath as a toddler starts wailing during dinner. Each round, jot a quick outcome in your daily log. Assign a relief score from 1 (still tense) to 10 (fully calm), write a line about what worked or blocked you, and note the environment—time, place, who was around. Use a template like: Cue → Action → Relief score → Barrier → Next tweak. Example: 'Pulse raced after email ping → 4-7-8 breathing → 6 → too many distractions at my desk → next time, turn away from screen.' This isn't about getting every detail perfect but collecting practical data on what helps you reset.

Expect tweaks. The first version of your plan may not fit a crowded train, a noisy office, or a moment when privacy vanishes. Try subtler actions when needed—like quietly pressing fingertips together instead of a full body stretch. Shorten actions under time crunches, squeezing in just ten seconds of slow breath rather than a two-minute tension scan. When cues are vague, make them more obvious by noting a specific phrase or sensation as your target. There's no shame in needing to modify plans; flexibility is the sign you're growing. Celebrate any adaptation—it means you're becoming skilled at self-support even when circumstances shift.

Sometimes, even the best plans can't be done in public or you're stuck without the right conditions. That's where backup moves come in. Have a simpler, more discreet fallback: silently count two full breaths, release only your jaw, or ground both feet firm on the floor. These micro-actions offer relief and keep you moving instead of freezing. Practice these backups once in advance so your mind can grab them easily when needed. You might realize subtle changes are all you need for real relief. Every action, even tiny ones, keeps you moving forward.

Learning to apply if–then plans in real situations is about staying curious and kind with yourself. Every cue noticed, action tried, and result logged is another step toward reliability under pressure. You're shifting from default reactions to actively shaping how you meet the world. Some days you'll hit your target, other days you'll miss—each is proof you're learning the cycle of adapting and improving. With a few rounds of experimenting and tweaking, you'll notice which habits lift you when stress spikes, while your toolbox gets easier and quicker to use. With these experiments as your lived foundation, you'll soon learn how to refresh, refine, and keep your plans serving you as life changes around you.

Keep Plans Alive

After seeing how if–then plans work in real moments, the key is making sure they don't gather dust. Once you've put your plans to the test, it's all about keeping them alive, not letting them slip into the background. Life keeps moving, new stressors pop up, and what worked last month may feel stale or mismatched by next quarter. This section walks through four action steps—monthly review, season shifts, visual cues, and the confidence loop—to help your emotional strategies stay sharp and ready, no matter what changes.

Monthly Review

A stable plan is a living tool. Set aside ten minutes each month for a quick 'If–Then Tune-Up.' Pick a day you're already doing some life maintenance—a bill-pay night, calendar sync, or Sunday prep. Pull out your list of if–then plans. Start by checking which ones you still notice in action. If you have a response that now happens automatically, mark it as 'archived'—it no longer needs daily attention. Then, look for plans you ignore or that feel confusing. Maybe a plan for morning overwhelm isn't helping because your mornings have changed. In that case, rewrite it or swap in a different one that fits current stress points. Simplifying complex or wordy plans matters here. A friction-free system lowers mental barriers.

Example: Replace "If I notice my chest tightening at 9am meetings, then I will close my eyes and visualize a waterfall for three minutes" with "If tension hits at 9am, then take 2 slow breaths." Shorter plans stick. With a monthly check-in, nothing lingers too long, and your strategies keep pace with your real life.

Season Shifts

Once your plans are up-to-date, think about seasonal changes that can throw curveballs. Travel, holidays, big project cycles, or school breaks often bring new triggers and old patterns. When you head into conference season or family holidays, your cues and action options shift—so your plans should, too (Noémie Van Maercke, 2025). Write travel-specific if–then plans, like "If I hear final boarding call, then I do a senses scan," or "If holiday stress builds, then I text one friend before reacting." Crunch times at work might call for plans such as "If my inbox passes 50 unread, then I set a ten-minute break timer." Each time a routine or environment shifts, refresh your plans so they act as reliable handles, not forgotten intentions. Anticipating these transitions makes adaptation smoother and stops old plans from failing when you need them most (Spreckley et al., 2021).

Visual Cues

With fresh plans on your list, focus on visibility. Reminders in sight make action automatic when pressure hits. Use sticky notes on monitors or above kitchen counters, fridge magnets, or even a lock screen image showcasing your most useful plan ("Pause + 2 breaths"). Set phone reminders labeled with the first step of the action instead of just "reminder," such as "Name the feeling, then sip water." Match cue placement to where your biggest triggers live: the car for commute stress, bathroom mirror for morning chaos, wallet for checkout nerves. Clear, visible cues fight decision fatigue and lighten your mental load when energy dips. The less you have to remember from scratch, the more likely you are to use your if-then plans in real time.

Confidence Loop

Layering positive feedback onto your system closes the gap between knowing and doing. Each time you run a plan—no matter how small—name it to yourself: "That was me choosing calm." Track streaks just seven days at a time, not forever. For every streak completed, pick a small reward: favorite playlist for your next drive, five quiet minutes outside, a quick text of your win to a friend or journal entry. These bite-sized rewards reinforce your identity as a person who handles stress with intention, not default reactivity. Over time, this builds self-trust and motivation to keep plans active.

With living, flexible if–then plans, calm starts to become your default—especially as you move toward stacking routines for even more reliable calm during tough transitions. This ongoing approach means your tools not only survive new challenges but actually get stronger through them.

Wrapping Up

By now, you've seen how stress can pop up in the most ordinary moments—a late ping, a sudden change, a memory that won't quit. What really changes the outcome is not just noticing those cues but stepping into a plan you've made ahead of time. If–then plans don't require you to be a different person or summon endless willpower; they're about having a clear path when your mind goes blurry. With just a bit of practice and some simple wording, these plans become a reliable shortcut to re-center yourself right as stress shows up, not hours later.

The beauty here is that every small action adds up. You're wiring new responses, experimenting, and tweaking as you go. Some days it will feel seamless, other times awkward, but that's the process of growth—messy, real, and fully human. As life shifts, so will your triggers and routines, but with a habit of checking in and updating your plans, you'll stay one step ahead of stress rather than playing catch-up. It's not about making stress disappear, but about meeting it with more calm, self-compassion, and choice each time it knocks on your door.

Chapter 8: Time-Limited Worry Window: Contain the Noise

Have you ever noticed how worrying can sneak in at the worst moments—like during an important meeting or right when you're trying to unwind? Trying to push those anxious thoughts away often feels like a losing battle, with worries popping up even more strongly. What if, instead of fighting those feelings all day long, you gave yourself permission to set aside a specific time just for them? Scheduling worry might sound unusual, but it's not about avoiding your concerns. It's about giving your mind a clear plan: there's a time and place where these thoughts get attention, so they don't have to interrupt everything else.

In this chapter, you'll discover how setting a dedicated 'worry window' can help contain mental noise and reduce that constant sense of urgency anxiety brings. You'll learn why putting worry on your calendar—not battling it head-on—is an effective approach. Step by step, we'll explore how to pick your worry slot, create boundaries that protect your day, and gently manage anxious thoughts without letting them take over. By the end, you'll be ready to turn worry from an uninvited guest into a scheduled visitor, giving your mind much-needed space to focus on what matters most.

Scheduling Worry Works

If you've ever tried to force worry away only to have it sneak back during a client call, bedtime, or the moment you want to focus most, you know how stubborn mental noise can be. Many high-achieving adults end up falling into a pattern of trying harder and harder to shove anxious thoughts aside— only to find them popping up more often, stealing peace from busy days and quiet nights. What if there's a way to pre-assign your worry a safe spot so it stops barging in all day long? The idea of scheduling time for worry might sound odd at first, but science shows that this approach is far from avoidance. Instead, it invites your brain to relax, knowing the concern will get proper attention soon.

The paradox of permission sits at the heart of why the worry window works. When you constantly try to push anxiety out of consciousness, your mind treats those worries as urgent— much like a child who tugs harder on your sleeve the more you ignore them. Suppression acts like a signal to the anxious brain: "This is dangerous, pay even more attention!" That's why forbidden thoughts tend to rebound stronger, often spilling over into meetings, commutes, or moments meant for rest. Yet when the brain knows worry is scheduled its own airtime, urgency drops. Instead of setting off red flags with every stray concern, the mind rests easier, holding off until the appointed slot. It discovers that worry doesn't need to run the show all day—there's a plan.

Applying boundaries brings another layer of relief. Think about how work meetings live on a calendar. When a topic has a set start and finish, there's less temptation to rehearse every point at random. Worry responds much the same way to containment. Give it a time slot, and intrusive loops lose their power to dominate every spare minute. This sense of structure is also known as stimulus control; it deals with training your attention so it doesn't leak into all areas of life. Imagine treating worry like email—if you have a routine time to check it, you aren't scanning your inbox every five minutes. Boundaries convert endless rumination into a managed appointment instead of a runaway process that zaps decision-making energy at the worst moments (Feldhaus et al., 2020).

Environmental cues may seem simple, but they hold surprising influence over your thought patterns. Using only one chair, notebook, or room for your worry window turns that specific spot into a trigger for allowed rumination—freeing up the rest of your world for other things. Say you always take calls in your office chair and use your journal at the kitchen table. If you only allow worrying in that one old armchair after dinner, you signal to your brain that spirals don't belong in bed, the car, or mid-conversation. This physical boundary helps retrain your nervous system, too—it becomes easier to step in and out of "worry mode" because repetition builds new associations. At first, this feels artificial or awkward. Sticking with the same routine, though, lets your brain adapt much faster than relying on willpower alone, since environmental consistency is one of the most reliable tools for changing ingrained habits (Feldhaus et al., 2020).

The benefits reach beyond the time you spend containing worry. There's a carryover calm effect that comes from practicing this kind of mental boundary-setting. When your brain learns that reminders will indeed be addressed at their scheduled session, it gradually trusts that it doesn't have to interrupt you while you work, parent, or try to sleep. These reduced pop-up alerts clear space for creative focus and steadier energy throughout packed days. For overloaded adults, this means fewer distractions, more room to solve problems, and evenings that feel less hijacked by unplanned rumination. Research supports that building containers for repetitive negative thoughts helps cut down overall arousal and enhances general well-being, even when some underlying stressors remain (Feldhaus et al., 2020; Tulbure et al., 2025).

Now that you've got the 'why' behind the worry window, next you'll learn how to pick your slot, set the rules, and start containing the noise—one concrete step at a time.

Set Your Daily Window

Boundaries for worry act like the walls of a room—creating space that protects everything else in your day. Knowing the science is only half the battle. You're now ready to build that mental room and put it into practice. It's normal to feel unsure at first. This exercise is for real lives, not perfect ones, and it works because it's flexible. Even showing up to set your window counts as progress, whether you use it for five minutes or the full block (Gupta, 2023).

Start by glancing over your usual day. Where does stress collect? When are you most likely to have privacy or at least a few quiet moments? Pick a slot that already fits, so you'll have less friction trying to stick with it. For some this could mean 5:30 pm before dinner, while others might find after the kids' bedtime more realistic. If you work late shifts, maybe lunchtime is your golden moment. The time doesn't have to be perfect; it just needs to be possible for most days. Put it on your calendar right now. Set a gentle phone alarm if that helps. Try something like, "right when I get home from work but before turning on the TV." If you tend to crash in the evening, pick a spot at least thirty minutes before bed—you want your sleep space to stay restful, not linked to worries (Gupta, 2023). Self-kindness is the vibe: you're not restricting yourself, just giving your mind a safe place to put anxiety down for a short stretch.

Location comes next. Choose a plain surface and basic chair—leave beds, couches, and desks out. Those carry sleep, relaxation, or work associations you don't want mixing with your worry window. Think hard chairs, stairs, or even a simple bench. If you share space or have limited room, get creative. A folding chair in the hallway or even a corner of the kitchen can work. What matters is consistency and neutrality—not perfection. Boring spots are good. They help you resist stretching out worry time longer than planned (Gupta, 2023). Store your worry notebook and pen there. The less effort needed to start, the more likely you'll keep going. If paper isn't an option today, set up a dedicated notes app on your phone—but try paper first, since it keeps boundaries clearer and distractions down.

Bring one notebook just for worry windows. Label it however you like—"Worry Room," "Anxiety Notes," or anything that feels both honest and private. Keep it in your chosen spot. Always have a pen there, too. Designate this one little book as your container. That way, your worries don't leak out everywhere else. Phone notes can step in for backup on especially busy days, but treat paper as your default for focus and emotional clarity.

Now for the window rules: only list what's worrying you. No problem-solving, research, or strategizing—not yet. During this window, write each worry down, then rate it on a simple scale from 0–10 for distress. This helps you spot which ones hit harder. Sometimes, urgent tasks will sneak in ("I need to email my boss!"). Just put a star next to those and move them to your to-do list once the window ends. Stay gentle and non-judging. You're learning what your mind wants to say, not forcing yourself to fix everything instantly.

Delaying worry outside the window will be its own skill. When an anxious thought intrudes at noon, calmly tell yourself, "I'll save this for 5:30 pm." Jot a quick phrase—maybe three words—on a sticky note or your phone: "worry—Monday meeting." Then move on. Every time you do this script, you're teaching your brain to trust the container. Even if it feels strange, stick with it. Monday's meeting pops back up at lunch? Repeat the script, log it briefly, and let yourself return to whatever you were doing. Expect doubts early on—almost everyone wonders if containment will really help. In practice, the repetition wires in a sense of safety and routine that starts to free up mental bandwidth (Gupta, 2023).

If anxiety is high or your schedule gets wild, keep your window short—five or ten minutes is plenty. Picking the time, place, and notebook and using the delay script once all count as solid wins. Small changes stack up, turning everyday busyness into an anchor point for calm. Schedule, show up, experiment, and remind yourself this isn't about perfection. It's about building a habit that protects your wellbeing (Gupta, 2023; *Routine Reset: Daily Habits for Good Mental Health | Psychology Today*, n.d.). Once your window is set, you'll be ready for the next section, where you'll learn exactly how to fill it using an easy three-column exercise tailored for true relief.

Apply Now: The Three-Column Page

By now, you've carved out a clear worry window in your day— a set block of time and a quiet spot just for sorting through anxious thoughts. It's time to make the most of that container, turning passing worries into something you can see, test, and manage. That's where the three-column page comes in. The act of writing slows down racing thoughts and gives each worry its own space. Instead of letting big fears swirl unchecked, you'll turn them into concrete statements and examine them side by side. This process takes hidden stressors—like replaying a tough conversation or dreading an upcoming deadline—and lays them out plainly, so they're less likely to nag you through the day.

Start by taking a blank sheet of paper or journal and drawing two vertical lines to create three columns. Label them "Worry," "Evidence," and "Next Step." Keep things simple—there's no right or wrong way to phrase what goes here. The point is honesty, not perfection. Have your timer ready to keep the window focused and short.

Column 1 – Worry

Write one worry per line using the plainest language possible. Don't filter, soften, or fix your words—this isn't a performance or an exercise in politeness. Pretend you're jotting down a quick note to yourself. After each worry, add a distress rating from 0 to 10. This helps track what's weighing on you most. Maybe you write, "I'll freeze during tomorrow's team presentation," then add a '7' if it feels pretty intense today. Or, "My friend hasn't texted back—I probably upset her," rated at '5.' Let every concern get its own spot; lumping them together only muddies the waters. By naming each one clearly, you shrink its power and get it out of your head and onto the page. Even if a worry feels embarrassing or overblown, write it anyway. These ratings aren't a grade—they're a guide for where your stress is centered today.

Column 2 – Evidence

Now take each worry and look for real-life facts, as if you're a reporter writing a news story. For every worry, ask: "What have I seen happen before? What proof do I have for and against this?" Be fair, but stick to facts, not gut feelings. If you're worried about stumbling over words in a meeting, list details like, "I practiced my slides twice," or "Last month I got positive feedback—even though I felt nervous." You might also note, "Did lose focus once when a question caught me off guard." If you can't find anything solid (say, it's a new scenario), just put a question mark and move along. No need to force cheerful spins: this column isn't about glossing over concerns but grounding them in reality. Sometimes just seeing how much—or how little—evidence is there can shift the emotional weight of a thought. This honest check-in moves anxiety from the realm of 'what if' into the world of 'what's actually true today?'

Column 3 – Next Step

In the last column, look at the evidence and write one clear action you could take now—or decide that watching and waiting is enough. The best steps are small, doable in less than ten minutes, or easy to schedule. Get specific: instead of "Get ready for meeting," write "Draft three speaking points," or "Review agenda with a colleague." For the earlier example about a friend, maybe your step is "Send a friendly text," or "Wait another day before reaching out." There will be times nothing needs doing; write "Observe" or "Let it sit." Grant yourself permission to drop worries that don't require immediate action—they aren't being ignored, just contained for now. By closing the loop, you create relief and momentum. Even a tiny next step turns anxious energy into forward movement.

Set your timer for 10–15 minutes as you work through your page. As soon as it rings, draw a horizontal line beneath your last entry. Physically close the notebook, stand up, and choose a brief cue—a stretch, a sip of water, or a walk to another room —to mark your return to regular life. If entries feel unfinished or worries still linger, trust that you have another window tomorrow. Over time, you'll notice some distress ratings start to drop, while others may stay the same. Both outcomes mean you're doing it right: the real progress lies in showing up, giving shape to anxious thoughts, and stepping away when the window closes.

Guardrails to Prevent Overrun: Reliable Cues and Gentle Course-Correction

After practicing the Three-Column Page journaling, many notice how giving worries a dedicated spot provides relief. Yet when life turns hectic or emotions run high, even the best worry windows can spill over. It's normal to have sessions that creep outside their boundaries. Rather than seeing this as failure, treat it like refueling your practice—these moments help shape your own maintenance manual.

A helpful first step is adding a hard stop alarm. Pick an unfamiliar tone for your timer—something you don't use for waking up, meetings, or reminders. The new sound serves as a clear "session done" cue, easing transition. Place your phone or timer across the room so you must physically stand to turn it off; movement helps shift gears mentally and signals closure (Schimming, 2022). When you hear the tone, let yourself end, even if you're mid-thought. If the session runs long, jot down what kept you there—maybe a stickier topic or a rough day. See this note as data, not a flaw. Tomorrow is another run, another chance.

Next comes the end-cap breath. Before closing your notebook or stepping away, try two rounds of breathing: inhale gently through the nose to a count of four, hold a moment, then exhale slowly through the mouth for six. Use each exhale to imagine releasing leftover tension from your mind and shoulders. Some prefer to add a small ritual—rolling the shoulders or standing in a forward fold for one breath—or even just tapping the pen on the notebook as a nod to completion. This physical reset anchors the end of your session in both body and mind. If thoughts linger, remind yourself: "I showed up. I get to move on now." You're not shoving worries away—just closing the book for today (Schimming, 2022).

If your list outgrows the session or you still have more worries waiting, the overflow rule steps in. After the alarm sounds, draw a solid line under what you wrote and label the next bit "Tomorrow." Any leftover concerns park here for a fresh start next time. Imagine it like rolling incomplete tasks into tomorrow's to-do list—wise pacing more than avoidance. Muscles get stronger from short, effective workouts with good rest; minds also thrive on contained effort and recovery (A Realistic Guide to Time Management, 2019).

Once a week, do a brief check-in with yourself about how this system is feeling. Skim your recent worry windows: How long did each actually last? Did any stretch past your set time? Make this a curious review, not a test. If you find windows running longer or leaking out, experiment by trimming the length for one week—try eight or ten minutes per session. You may find shorter, sharper focus gives more relief and less fatigue. Resetting timers or moving back toward lighter structure is part of skill-building, not starting over.

Keep an eye out for small markers of progress: Did you respect the session's end? Did you use your alarm, or pause for a breath before leaving your spot? Each bit counts as proof you're strengthening this practice. Whether you're running three-minute windows or navigating overflow days, you're still in the game. Every tweak is a chance to protect your energy and keep containment feeling safe. Guardrails are gentle companions, not rigid rulers, always ready to be adjusted as needed.

Boundaries help turn worry time into something light and reliable, less likely to spiral or leave you wrung out. These protective cues make space for calm, even on rough days. Up next, you'll learn how to close each window with calming, body-based scripts—the next step in keeping boundaries supportive and your container strong. (A Realistic Guide to Time Management, 2019; Schimming, 2022)

Final Thoughts

Learning to schedule time for worry is about more than just managing anxious thoughts—it's about making space for yourself in the middle of a busy life. Setting aside a few minutes each day, in a specific spot, creates a simple structure where worries can show up and be heard, without taking over every moment. By writing things down and using tools like the three-column page, you give your mind a clear signal: it's okay to have concerns, but they don't need to run on loop all day long. Just having this plan in place helps reduce that nagging urgency, so you can get back to work, rest, or whatever else matters most—knowing there's a safe zone waiting when you really need it.

If your window runs over or if worries sneak outside their time slot, remember that's completely normal. The system is meant to be flexible, not perfect. Short sessions, gentle resets, and small steps all count as progress. With practice, these boundaries start to feel natural, helping you reclaim energy and focus bit by bit, even on tough days. What matters most is showing up, being kind to yourself, and letting the routine do the heavy lifting. This isn't about eliminating worry forever—

it's about giving it a place, so it stops crowding out joy, rest, and everyday calm.

Chapter 9: Boundary Scripts: Protect Your Energy in Real Time

Ever find yourself stuck, scrambling to find the right words when you need to say no or set a limit? Moments like these can spike your stress because your nervous system is reacting faster than your brain can craft a perfect response. That's where nervous-system-smart boundaries come in—short, clear scripts that act as quick tools to protect your energy and keep your body calm in real time. These aren't long-winded explanations or apologies; they are simple, kind phrases designed to help you pause, breathe, and respond without feeling overwhelmed or reactive.

This chapter will walk you through ready-to-use boundary scripts tailored for those pressure-filled moments, paired with delivery skills to help your message land calmly and confidently. You'll learn why keeping boundaries brief and neutral supports not just others' understanding but also your own emotional regulation. By practicing these scripts and ways of saying them, you'll gain reliable tools that make protecting your time and energy feel natural, even when life gets hectic.

Nervous System-Smart Boundaries: How Short Scripts Lower Stress in Real Time

Self-awareness and emotional skills built earlier are your body's first line of defense against stress. Boundaries add a second layer, acting like a shield that not only communicates where you stand but also keeps your nervous system from hitting overload. When demands pile up—endless emails, late-night texts, last-minute meeting requests—it's easy for reactivity to set in, leaving you anxious or resentful long after the moment passes. Instead of just gritting your teeth or apologizing through another boundary cross, short, clear scripts help your brain and body downshift into calm.

When pressure spikes, decision-making and emotional capacity shrink. The more tired or overwhelmed you feel, the harder it becomes to form new sentences, let alone maintain composure. This is why short, kind boundary scripts matter—they act as simple shortcuts for your mind. Think of them like emergency instructions: easy to remember, always ready. Imagine getting a work message at 8 p.m. when you're already exhausted. Rather than scrambling for what to say, you use, "Thanks for thinking of me! I'm off for the night—catch you tomorrow." You might notice your shoulders drop or your breath slow as relief sets in. Before replying, try one slow exhale and silently rehearse your script. Even this tiny pause drops adrenaline and gives your body space to respond instead of react.

Clarity beats apology every time. Long-winded, apologetic explanations often invite counterarguments, pushback, or even more requests. "I'm really sorry, I wish I could, but…" can sound soft to others and feels shaky inside. In contrast, phrases like "That doesn't work for me, thanks for understanding" create a no-negotiation zone. Picture declining an extra project with your boss or telling your parent you can't make dinner. The conversation ends faster; you spend less energy replaying what happened later. Using short, neutral language isn't rude—it's a kindness to your nervous system and theirs. It lets everyone know where things stand without blame or guilt, making future repeats easier. You know it's working when you find yourself ruminating less or stop feeling tense hours after setting a limit.

Pre-written wins set you up for pressure moments. In the thick of things, adrenaline narrows your vocabulary, sometimes freezing words altogether. It's common to blank on what to say or default to yes out of habit. Preparing phrases ahead of time—typed in your phone's notes app, written on a sticky note at your desk, or even rehearsed aloud—makes recall automatic. Try this: write one go-to line for tricky asks and practice it once today. It could be, "Let me check my calendar and get back to you," or simply, "I can't right now." Repetition primes your mouth so the words come out before anxiety does. Early wins aren't dramatic; catching a pause before responding, or using your script once, counts. Each success tells your brain it's safe to keep setting boundaries, even if it feels awkward at first.

Consistency is your friend. Whether you're at work, texting family, or chatting with friends, repeating the same phrase helps your brain autopilot boundaries. Default responses—"I need to pass, but thank you"—start to feel familiar and less scary over time. In mixed teams or diverse households, you might tweak the tone or words, but the core stays the same. At first, you may worry it's robotic or cold, but this fades quickly. What matters is how you feel after: less churn, quicker recovery, more ease.

Try starting small. Pick one area—a group chat, a recurring work ask—and choose a single script. Notice any physical signals: does your jaw unclench, breath deepen, or mind wander less afterward? If you freeze or stumble the first few tries, that's normal. Every attempt is a signal to your nervous system that you're safe to draw a line. With this groundwork on why short, neutral scripts support both communication and stress regulation, you're ready for the next step. Now that you know why short, neutral scripts help your nervous system and communication, we'll build your personal script set for common pressure points.

Create Your Script Set

Short, calm scripts are now at your fingertips. The next move is to make sure those words fit your life and give you backup when old habits or pressure take over. Scripts work best when they feel familiar—like tools kept in a well-worn pocket. When the stress hits, you'll have something steady to lean on instead of freezing or falling into people-pleasing. Each of these script types targets moments that often trip up even the most capable adults. What matters most is shaping them so they sound like you—and practicing until they stick.

Time Guard: Protecting Your Schedule and Priorities

A "Time Guard" script helps you manage workload and time, whether a last-minute project appears at work or a friend asks for impromptu plans. These scripts let you pause instead of saying yes right away. For many, the slippery slope starts with small requests adding up to late nights or lost weekends. A good Time Guard gives you a clear line without sounding harsh.

Script Purpose:
Protects your focus and energy; decreases overload from unexpected demands.

Building Steps:
1. Start with, "Let me check my calendar and get back to you."
2. State a realistic revisit time: "I'll let you know by tomorrow morning."
3. Practice a brief version for true emergencies: "Can I confirm in 10 minutes?"

Examples:

- Work: Manager sends you an email: "Can you turn this around tonight?" You reply, "I want to give this proper focus. Let me check my other deadlines and get back to you by noon."
- Social: Friend texts, "Drinks after work?" You respond, "Tonight's packed, but let me see if I can shift things and text you in an hour."

Notice how both end with a clear next step, taking pressure off the moment. Choose revisit times that fit real life—if it's always 'five minutes,' it loses power. If someone pushes back, repeat your line. Most find it easier to remember and less tiring than saying yes then regretting it later.

Progress Indicator:

If you remember to use even a rough draft once this week, that's real progress. It feels smoother each time as you hear yourself say it aloud.

Pause Button: Creating Space Before Answering

Some situations leave little room to think—a manager waiting for a response, a tense family text thread, a teacher requesting help after school. The "Pause Button" brings air into tense conversations. Its job is to create a buffer, putting some distance between you and the demand so adrenaline doesn't take over.

Script Purpose:

Gives instant breathing room, checks emotional state, enables thoughtful choices.

Building Steps:

1. Pick a go-to phrase: "I need a moment to think about that."
2. Add a timeframe: "Can I circle back after lunch?"
3. Save a shortcut on your phone: type out "Can I come back to you later today?" as a draft text or quick-reply.

Examples:

- Office: Coworker says, "Could you cover my meeting in 10 minutes?" You answer, "Let me review what's on my plate. Can I let you know by 3:00?"
- Home: Partner asks about taking on extra weekend chores. You text, "I need a sec to look at our schedule. I'll confirm after dinner."

The key is naming the exact time you'll decide and taking those few extra breaths. This also signals respect for yourself and others—you're not vanishing or stalling, just giving the question its due attention. Early tries may feel awkward, but quick script use reduces regret later.

Progress Indicator:

If you use the Pause Button at all, you're building new muscle. Over time, pausing gets easier and less nerve-wracking.

Scope Check: Clarifying What's Being Asked

Requests sometimes come loaded with vague expectations or hidden tasks. A "Scope Check" script helps set what you're actually being asked to do—so you don't volunteer for everything just to be polite.

Script Purpose:
Clarifies priorities before committing, prevents confusion or silent overload.

Building Steps:
1. Respond with a clarifying question: "Are you asking for just the slides, or the full report too?"
2. Focus on one thing: "What's the top priority here?"
3. If timing is fuzzy, pin down timing: "When do you need this by?"

Examples:
- Office: Two bosses ask, "Can you handle these?" Say, "So I'm clear—do you want both projects finished before Friday, or just started?"
- Volunteer group: Organizer says, "Can you help with planning?" Respond, "Is that organizing snacks, or leading activities?"

This shifts responsibility for clarity back where it belongs—on the request—not on you to guess or absorb extra without knowing. If someone can't clarify, you can always say, "Let me know when you're sure what's needed. Happy to help within my limits."

Progress Indicator:
You may notice less dread or second-guessing before saying yes. If the scope feels clear, you're on track.

No Without Guilt: Saying No Warmly and Briefly

"No Without Guilt" helps you say no without apologizing or over-explaining. Most people tie themselves in knots here. Keeping it short reduces chances for pushback and cuts mental fatigue.

Script Purpose:
Lets you honor limits clearly; preserves relationships without self-sacrifice.

Building Steps:
1. Start with "No" or "I can't this time."
2. End warmly: "Thanks for understanding."
3. Offer an alternative only if you truly mean it ("Maybe next week?"). No need to justify.

Examples:
- Work: Colleague says, "Could you stay late again?" You say, "No, I can't do extra hours today. Hope the rest of your evening goes smoothly."
- Personal: Family member asks for help moving last minute. You reply, "I'm not available today, but I hope it goes smoothly."

Early attempts can spark guilt—that's common. Each try, the ground gets a little steadier underfoot. Using notes or reminders supports the learning curve.

Progress Indicator:
If you say no, even once, without launching into reasons, count that as a strong step forward. Clarity is progress, not perfect comfort.

With your scripts drafted, the next step is delivery—how you breathe, speak, and hold your body so the message lands without escalation.

Apply Now: Delivery Under Stress

With your scripts ready, let's practice how to deliver them under pressure. Earlier, you've taken time to develop self-awareness and created practical scripts for tricky moments. The next step is putting that language into action, even when emotions are high and the room feels tense. Practicing real-time delivery closes the gap between knowing what to say and actually saying it—this is how boundaries move from paper to life. When stress rises, our bodies react first; skills like breathwork, steady tone, and grounded body language help anchor you so your words sound clear and confident (workingoncalm, 2025).

Picture a situation: Your boss asks if you can "just squeeze in one more project" late on a Friday. Or, a relative shows up last minute expecting help. Even seasoned script writers can freeze or stumble here. That's why practice matters. You want your boundary to come out as calmly as it sounded in your head. Every technique here can be tried in private before sharing it in real life—and every try counts, wobbles and all.

Start with breath plus speech. The moment before you say your boundary, allow yourself a pause. Inhale gently through your nose. Exhale slowly, counting down—three, two, one. On the next soft inhale, start speaking your boundary. This slow breath cues your body to settle and steadies your voice. Repeat the same breath cycle if you feel your nerves rising mid-sentence. For text or email, pause before typing, let your shoulders drop, and reread before sending. Taking these few seconds can save energy and add clarity (workingoncalm, 2025).

Tone carries more meaning than most words, especially when stakes are high. Warmth doesn't mean lack of firmness—it signals confidence and calm. Practice by recording yourself reading a script at a bedtime-story pace. Stop at each period, letting the sentence breathe. Avoid tacking on apologies or over-explaining. If someone pushes back, repeat your line at the same speed with the same warmth. Try: "I won't be able to add this to my plate right now." If someone asks again, calmly restate: "As I said, I can't take this on." Keeping a steady pace avoids escalation and guards your energy (workingoncalm, 2025).

Your posture also speaks. Stand or sit with feet solid on the floor. Soften your jaw and drop your shoulders. Keep your chin level and eyes forward. These cues help convince your own nervous system that things are safe and can keep others from misreading hesitation as uncertainty. For digital boundaries, break up your message with line breaks or bold print for key points, making it easy to read and hard to overlook. If urgency comes up, short sentences with white space give your message quiet authority.

Many people fear what happens if someone keeps pressing after a boundary is delivered. Practice repeating the same script once, word-for-word. Then stop. If more pressure comes, have a backup phrase like "I've shared my plan—talk soon," which keeps you from being drawn in further. Knowing this in advance helps you stay in control and signals the conversation is closed without sounding harsh (workingoncalm, 2025).

Practicing out loud, in front of a mirror, or by sending yourself a voice memo adds muscle memory, making it easier when tension hits. Set a timer—practice each skill for just a minute or two at a time. Jot down how it feels afterwards to track progress, not perfection. Adrenaline spikes, clumsy sentences, and awkward pauses all count as practice. Each try makes the next easier. Use gentler versions of scripts if you're new, like "That won't work for me," and level up to direct ones when ready. Text and email versions also count—boundary-setting happens across all formats (workingoncalm, 2025).

Remind yourself that adrenaline may jump in right after you deliver a boundary. That's your cue that you're building a new skill, not a sign of failure. Safety matters most—if anything feels unsafe or shaky, pause and take care of yourself.

After you deliver a boundary, adrenaline can linger. Next, we'll cover aftercare and quick resets so you recover and refine your delivery skills.

Aftercare and Adjustments

After you deliver a boundary—even perfectly—nervous energy and doubts can linger. These moments matter as much as the conversation itself. Your body may still carry the adrenaline from saying no, your thoughts might race with guilt or second-guessing. Turning these aftershocks into recovery time is the next step in making new responses feel natural, not forced. The methods here are designed to fit into the busiest workday or family schedule—quiet tools that help you reset, adjust, and grow. You now have the language, delivery, and recovery steps to protect your energy. Keep these scripts visible for the next week and practice once daily to make them your new default.

Try This: Shake It Out

Boundary-setting is taxing because it kicks off a real stress response in your nervous system. Even when your words come out just as planned, your muscles can lock up or tingle. To finish the stress cycle, stand if you can. Quickly shake out one arm, then the other, alternating back and forth ten to fifteen times. Then switch to each leg—no marathon moves, just firm flicks like brushing off water. If standing isn't an option, do calf raises at your desk or give both hands a brisk shake under the table. Each shake-out ends with a long, slow exhale, shoulders lowering as you breathe. For privacy, the restroom works well. This trick bumps you back into calm when your body tries to stay on alert. Picture closing your laptop right after telling a team lead, "I'm not available to take this on." You duck into the hallway, do thirty seconds of movement, and return feeling less jagged.

Try This: Self-Compassion Line

After holding a boundary, guilt or self-criticism often surfaces —especially for high-achievers who fear letting others down. Flipping this script helps build resilience. Put your hand on your chest. In a quiet tone, say, "It's okay to protect my time." Repeat three times. Notice the warmth of your hand, the steadiness of your breath. If the old guilt grabs hold, try finishing this sentence on paper: "By saying no to this, I'm saying yes to..." Fill it in honestly—maybe rest, focus, or even sanity. This moment acts as a circuit-breaker for self-blame. Think about turning down an extra project even though someone else wanted your help. Whisper this line as you walk back to your office, reminding yourself that saving quiet evenings lets you show up better for those you love and for yourself (Nash, 2018).

Try This: Debrief Note

Review makes new habits stick. Right after the interaction, jot two quick notes in your phone or notebook. First, the "keeper phrase"—the part of your script that landed well and felt true. Second, something to "tweak for next time"—what could be clearer, shorter, or calmer. For instance, maybe you told a manager, "I'm at capacity right now," but saw confusion on their face. Your keeper: "At capacity". Your tweak: Next time, add, "Let's check back in next Friday." Doing this creates a growing menu of phrases and adjustments you can use— including ones tailored for friends, parents, bosses, or chat groups. Over time, reading through your list turns uncertainty into a sense of command. Keeping a running doc called "Boundary Scripts" gives busy people a quick reference for real-world situations (Nash, 2018).

Try This: Escalation Plan

No matter how exact your script, sometimes others push back. Having a next-step ready cuts down on panic or flustered replies. Pair every key boundary with a backup statement that's firmer but not harsh. An example: You say, "I can't join the meeting after five." If asked again, reply, "I'm not available for this. Please proceed without me." Decide beforehand whether to move the interaction to email for documentation if requests keep coming. In personal life, consider setting your own consequence—like declining all new invitations for a certain period if boundaries go ignored.

Picture declining a friend's third last-minute dinner invite after already explaining your need for downtime. You simply repeat your script and propose a phone call later that week instead. At work, respond to another nudge for weekend availability by replying in writing rather than verbally—putting the break on emotional ping-pong. Upfront planning protects your energy without creating fresh drama (Nash, 2018; Tawwab, 2021, p. 130).

Practice Tips That Fit Busy Lives

Try these exercises whenever you need to recover—not just in private or perfect settings. Shake out tension during breaks between meetings, whisper your self-compassion line while tidying your workspace, and review your keeper phrases before bed. Small tweaks add up. Seeing stumbles as normal shrinks shame and builds trust in your ability to recover quickly. Every repetition inches you closer to boundaries being your steady state, not a special effort. Reflection links wins to habit—making boundary-setting less like a script and more like second nature. With recovery and adjustment solidified, you're set up for even deeper agency as you reshape habits and anchor calm in the chapters to come.

Final Thoughts

Setting boundaries in real time doesn't have to be complicated or draining. By having short, clear scripts that you've practiced and made your own, you can step into stressful moments with more calm and confidence. These ready-to-use lines aren't about being rigid or distant—they're a way to preserve your energy, keep your mind clearer, and help your nervous system settle instead of spiral. With just a few words, you transform tense situations into manageable ones and make it easier to recover afterward. The more you use these scripts, the more natural they'll feel, and over time, your brain and body will get better at recognizing what feels okay and when to pause, clarify, or say no.

Remember, it's normal to feel awkward or a bit guilty at first, but every attempt is progress—each small win adds up. Boundary-setting is a skill; the more you practice, tweak, and reflect, the steadier you become. Whether you're juggling work, family, or friends, having these scripts and delivery tools close by can make a huge difference in how you move through pressure points. As you build your set, keep practicing the delivery and paying attention to what works for you. Protecting your energy is not only possible—it gets easier each time you draw a clear line.

Chapter 10: Habit Loop Rewrite: Install Calm as Default

Imagine waking up in the next month to a morning that feels calm, even when your schedule is packed from start to finish. Your phone buzzes with messages and notifications, but instead of that familiar rush of anxiety creeping in, your body stays relaxed—shoulders soft, breath steady. Life still throws unexpected challenges your way—a surprise meeting, a tricky text to respond to—but you move through them differently now. You catch yourself in a rhythm: pause, breathe, let go, and then make a choice. What once used to drag your focus down an endless spiral now clears away in minutes, leaving space for energy and clarity at the close of each day.

This new sense of calm isn't a lucky break or a passing mood; it's something your habits keep rewiring into your everyday life. To create this shift, we'll explore how to turn all those scattered techniques you've tried into a consistent, dependable system. By understanding how the signals around you (cues), the actions you take (routines), and the feelings or benefits you get (rewards) work together, you can reshape how you respond to stress and build calm as your default setting—no matter what the day throws your way.

From Tools to System: Building a Reliable Habit Loop for Everyday Calm

Up to this point, you've collected helpful tools for stress management. Maybe you've tried a quick breathing exercise after work, or jotted down a grounding phrase to repeat during tense meetings. Still, without a clear system, these wins may show up randomly and then slip away. Building a reliable habit loop is how you can move from scattered experiments to feeling calm as your default—not just on lucky days but every day, no matter how hectic things get.

A habit loop has three main parts: cue, routine, and reward (Harvey et al., 2021). When you connect these together consciously, you shift from reacting on autopilot to living with intention—even in the middle of modern chaos. You'll start by finding your stress triggers, swap in calming routines, line up rewards that actually feel good, and start tracking progress, all with your real-world pressures in mind.

Cue Audit: Spot the Real Triggers

Identifying what sets off your stress spiral makes change possible. These moments are not failures—they're like storm warnings that help you plan ahead. Begin by listing five situations that most often start your stress response. Look for things like "reading emails first thing," "evening arguments with a partner," or "scrolling on social media when tired." Be as specific as possible; this shows you exactly where new routines can make a difference.

Track body cues too—jaw clenching, butterflies in your stomach, shallow breathing, or the urge to check your phone. Over the next week, use your phone or planner to jot down what triggers you noticed and when. Try color-coding times and locations on your calendar for quick reference. Don't judge yourself if you catch only a few at first; just spotting them is progress. Think of this as tracking the weather, not stopping it—you're building awareness without blame.

Routine Swap: Simple Moves for New Responses

The trigger is only half the story; what comes after is where lasting change happens. The routine is your automatic move when the cue hits. Changing this doesn't mean dramatic overhaul. Small, steady swaps become more reliable than once-in-a-while big gestures. Next to each cue on your list, pick a short calming tool you've already learned—two box breaths, quietly naming three things you can see, or relaxing your jaw and rolling your shoulders. Keep it short and doable, even on your busiest days.

Create a reminder script for every swap, such as "Breathe first, then answer" or "Relax jaw, then open email." Place prompts where you'll see them right before your trigger moments: phone lock screens, post-its on your laptop, water bottle labels, or calendar alerts. Practice one swap daily during calm moments, not just when stressed, so the move feels familiar when real chaos hits.

Reward Fit: Make Reinforcement Real

You might think rewards belong to kids or training pets, but your nervous system responds best to these instant positives. They don't need to be extravagant—a sunny glance out the window, a microstretch, sipping your favorite coffee, listening to a song clip, or giving a pet a quick scratch are all strong options. Link your reward to finishing your calming move—not to having full control or a perfect mood. Your brain connects the reward with the new behavior, making it easier to stick.

Rotate rewards every few days to prevent boredom. Pay attention to which ones leave you more refreshed or grounded. Even five seconds is enough for reinforcement. This isn't childish—it's smart brain science for grownups (Harvey et al., 2021).

Track Signals: Notice Wins and Adjust Gently

Real results show up as small improvements: catching tension early, feeling less wiped out, or rebounding faster after hard moments. Use a simple tension score from 0–10 before and after your new calming routine. Log this in a notebook or app, along with notes like "caught myself sooner" or "quit scrolling five minutes earlier than last time."

Try tracking latency (how quickly you spot a cue) and duration (how long distress lasts). Add where you made everyday gains —sending a tough message early, stepping away from work drama, catching your breath before responding. If logging daily seems like too much, set a twice-weekly check-in instead. Remember, this isn't a test—it's evidence that little wins add up. Celebrate any step forward, including simply noticing more than yesterday.

With your core habit loop visible, you'll soon begin designing a stacked sequence to anchor calm throughout your day. Linking these loops together will help turn smoother emotional regulation into a natural part of your everyday routine. That's where we're headed next.

Design Your Calm Chain: Linking Anchor Routines Into Real Life

By now, you've tracked the habit loops running through your day—those moments where cue leads to reaction and then reward. You know what sets off stress, which calming routines bring relief, and what feels rewarding afterwards. You even have a list of go-to techniques that soothe anxiety in small bursts or slow down a racing mind (Amen Clinics, 2025; Bentley et al., 2023). This section will help you turn those single tools into a connected, real-world chain—building small, repeatable rituals at predictable points so calm becomes less of a random bonus and more of an automatic part of your routine.

Morning Anchor: Set Your Signal Early

Start your chain by anchoring a calming practice right where your day begins. The aim is to greet the day with intention, not jump into autopilot. For some, this means a five-minute breathing session before the phone comes out. For others, it might be stretching at the foot of the bed or writing three quick morning intentions while coffee brews. If mornings already feel rushed, don't force a new seated meditation; instead, tie your anchor to something already happening—like taking three deep breaths every time you step into the shower or press the kettle button. Try placing a dot sticker on your bathroom mirror or coffee mug as a gentle reminder. Check in with yourself after: are shoulders lower? Is your breath slower? Even a one-minute conscious pause counts.

Steps for a Quick Morning Calm

1. Pick one easy spot (mirror, shower, mug).
2. Choose a calming act you like (breathwork, stretch, mini-intention).
3. Add a reminder (sticker, note, alarm tone).
4. Notice one thing different (less jaw tension, steadier mood).

Midday Reset: Find Your Pressure Valve

Lunch hours and midmorning breaks are natural pressure points. Midday, try another small "reset" ritual to punctuate stress before it piles up. If work gets busy, turn your water-bottle refill or bathroom trip into a calm anchor: as you fill your glass, pause for two rounds of box breathing or clench and release your fists. For parents or caregivers, the moment a child naps or puts on a show can work—stand by the window, notice the sky, and name something you're grateful for. If working from home, use the time after a meeting ends—just two minutes, eyes closed, floods your system with calm rather than racing on to the next task (Amen Clinics, 2025).

Steps for an At-Desk or On-the-Go Reset

1. Identify your usual pause (bathroom break, bottle refill, post-call sigh).
2. Pair it with a short calm action (breathing, stretch, gratitude thought).
3. Track if you feel less tense before lunch or able to focus better during afternoon slumps.

Afternoon Grounding: Transition Rituals That Stick

Afternoons often trigger fatigue or anxious thoughts. To prevent spirals, slip a grounding routine into the transition between work and evening—or right before the pre-dinner scramble. This could be standing near a window for three minutes of mindful breathing, taking a brisk walk around the block, or tracing a slow circle on your palm with a finger. For those in public or open offices, slow rhythmic breathing at your desk works fine. Place a sticky note on your monitor reading "exhale" or set a silent phone alarm as a private nudge. If you miss your anchor, try again tomorrow—progress builds across attempts, not perfection.

Quick Steps for Afternoon Grounding

1. Choose a spot or recurring event (end of a call, commute start, child's homework time).
2. Practice a moving anchor (walking, breathing, light stretch, tactile focus).
3. Jot down in a notes app when you caught yourself using the anchor.

Evening Release: Let Worry Go Before Rest

Calm ramps down gently in the evening if you set a finish line for ruminating. Try a "worry window": give yourself five minutes to write concerns, then close the notebook or phone and move on. Or end the day with a wind-down routine like legs-up-the-wall pose, slow 4-7-8 breathing, or quietly naming three things that went well. Shift the anchor to wherever feels doable—on the couch, bedside, or in the bath. Remind yourself there's no badge for doing every step daily—the win is returning when you notice tension building (Bentley et al., 2023; Amen Clinics, 2025).

Easy Evening Calm Routine Steps

1. Pick your shutdown time (after dinner, pre-bed, just before TV).
2. Use a brief ritual (worry window, gentle movement, reflecting gratitude).
3. Note one benefit—maybe sleep comes faster or the mind softens before lights out.

It's normal to miss a link or swap practices as life shifts. Customize timing, locations, and actions for your needs. Maybe shift the noon anchor to late morning or stack two mini-practices together after a rough meeting. Small, steady repetitions anchor calm deeper each week. With a day-long chain mapped, it's time to test and tweak in short cycles so the system fits your real life.

Apply Now: Weekly Experiment Cycle

With your customized daily calm routine mapped out, you're ready for the stage that actually makes it stick— experimentation. This isn't about overhauling your life overnight. Change happens best when you work with curiosity, not urgency. Think of this as a weekly cycle for tweaking habits in real settings to see what works for your actual, unpredictable life.

Pick One Variable

Choose one tiny shift. Change either the timing or the technique of a calming habit—never both at once. This makes feedback clear and keeps things doable. For example, move your morning breath from before coffee to right after you wake up. Swap the evening muscle release for a two-minute stretch if you're feeling more restless than tense. Stick with this single adjustment for one workweek—five days. Resist the urge to assess too soon. At the end of each day, jot down what felt easier and what popped up as a roadblock. You are tracking, not scoring yourself. If you miss a day or two, log it honestly and notice the pattern without self-blame.

Example:

- Monday: Swapped box breathing to just before the commute. Found it easier with fewer distractions.
- Wednesday: Forgot entirely amidst school drop-off scramble.
- Friday: Did a brief version in the car. Not perfect, but stuck with it.

Measure Relief

Each day, check tension levels like you would steps on a fitness tracker. Rate your mental or physical tension from 0 (completely calm) to 10 (max tension) right before your habit and again two minutes after. Note what you notice—did your shoulders relax? Did your mind race less? Throw in a quick tag for context—morning dread, work emails, after dinner logistics. Use any method that fits: write it on your phone notes, start a tracker page in your notebook, or put one sticky note on the fridge per day with a simple up or down arrow.

Example:

- Before habit: 7 (prepping for a big meeting)
- After habit: 4 (notice slower breathing, less jaw tightness)

Adjust for Reality

Life will throw you curveballs—a double-booked afternoon, a kid meltdown, surprise deadlines. The cycle expects chaos, not order. Each morning, do a quick self-check: ask, "Heavy, medium, or light day?" Match your habit version. Micro-version: one mindful breath, single shoulder roll, or thirty seconds of stillness when you have no time. Deluxe version: full guided relaxation, longer stretch, or soothing playlist after work. Missed days or incomplete tries aren't failures—they're reminders of what your nervous system needs next week.

Adaptation Examples:

- Micro: One slow breath while you microwave lunch.
- Deluxe: Ten-minute full body scan after tough meetings.

- Family version: Two minutes of quiet music before dinner as a group reset.

Celebrate Evidence

Give yourself a Friday check-in. List three shifts or wins from your week—small or big. Maybe "paused scrolling for one deep breath," "walked into dinner less tense," or "answered a tough email without stewing." Write them out, text a friend, or note them in your journal. Celebrate with something pleasant—a favorite song, a fresh cup of coffee, or a step outside. These wins prove change is happening, even when it feels minor. Progress cues might sound like: "I caught myself before spiraling," "My neck isn't as stiff at bedtime," "I actually started looking forward to my morning anchor."

What to Expect Next

Setbacks and weird weeks will happen. Relapses aren't the opposite of growth. They're built into the process. Next up, you'll learn how to shield your new calm habits from stress spikes and routine hiccups—so your system stays strong, even when life gets bumpy.

Handling Habit Dips, Upgrades, and Reviews: Keeping Calm Your Default in Real Life

Once your weekly experiment cycle is in motion, it's time to set up a safety net so you're prepared when routines wobble and life gets busy. Everyone hits a dip now and then. High-achievers like you often feel a gut-punch if calm routines slide, even for a few days. That doesn't mean you've failed—it's just how change works. Think of emotional growth like a spiral, not a straight line. Sometimes you circle back to old stress responses. It's normal. One simple move? Write a precommitment note on a sticky or your phone: "A dip means recalibrate, not start over." Keep this in sight—on your desk, mirror, laptop, wherever you pass by most.

Let yourself zoom out. Even after travel, illness, work crunches, or family curveballs, you can restart with the smallest version of calm—a 'minimum viable calm' practice. This might be a single slow breath before hitting send on an edgy email, or two minutes of silence with your coffee before jumping into the day. These micro-moves aren't consolation prizes; they're powerful anchors. When routines get knocked off course, block 20 minutes on your calendar as a dedicated reset window. Use that time to do only one small, familiar calming habit. The goal is to lower the threshold for feeling "back on track" so momentum rebuilds without guilt.

Next comes the emergency kit, your real-life insurance for high-stress moments. Build your kit around two tools you'll actually use and can grab instantly. These should be fast, visible, and take no prep. Maybe it's a smooth stone for grounding, a mantra written on your lock screen, or a 60-second breathing video saved in your favorites. Store them where you hit friction: next to your keyboard, on your nightstand, in your pocket. The easier they are to see, the more likely you'll use them. When things get shaky, try this two-step script: "Pause and breathe. Then choose one next step." That moment to slow down interrupts spirals and lets you respond, not react. Before a meeting, during a tense text exchange, or when you notice your jaw tightening, let your emergency kit anchor you back to center.

To make calm routines last, quarterly reviews come next. Think of this like swapping out clothes with the season—not a judgment, just an update. Schedule a fifteen-minute review date every quarter. Pull up your list of cues (triggers) and routines. Does anything feel stale or mismatched to life right now? Maybe you started running early mornings but now need a before-bed wind-down. Swap, delete, or add as needed. Next, look at your if–then plans. Archive what worked into a one-page 'Calm SOP'—a standard operating procedure for yourself. Use bullet points: 'If stress spikes after lunch, then walk outside.' This cheat sheet becomes your reference when energy dips or new stressors show up. Celebrate anything that stuck—even if all you did was pause once a day. If you can put this date on your calendar now, you're ahead of the game.

The last piece is mapping your habits to values. Sticking with routines has less to do with willpower and more to do with what matters to you right now. Choose just two values that light you up this season—maybe presence, playfulness, growth, connection, or creativity. Tag each current habit with the value it supports. This keeps your why clear when motivation slumps. Then pick one calm upgrade for the quarter. It could be 'no phone for twenty minutes before bed to protect rest,' or 'start meetings with two breaths to model calm leadership.' Make it small and specific. Each week, check in with yourself: 'Did this habit help me live my value of presence (or connection)?' Make tweaks as you go. Perfection isn't the goal—alignment is.

Keep your system lightweight, flexible, and personal. Treat calm routines like living things: let them breathe, evolve, and fit whatever life sends your way. By normalizing dips, planning emergency resets, reviewing gently, and tying habits to values, you turn uncertain experiments into reliable anchors. As you move forward, keep your habit system flexible, lightweight, and dialed in to what you care about most—let calm feel personal, not perfect.

Bringing It All Together

Stepping back, you've learned how to turn scattered calming techniques into a steady system that fits right into your real life. With cues, routines, and rewards working together, calm doesn't have to be a lucky accident or just wishful thinking on busy days. Instead, you can rely on habits that support you through early mornings, stressful emails, surprise meetings, and even the evening wind-down. You now have flexible ways to track small wins, adjust when life throws curveballs, and even restart smoothly after those inevitable dips. Each time you practice a calming move, you're adding strength to the foundation—bit by bit, it really does get easier and more automatic.

The most important takeaway is this: calm is not about perfection or hustling harder. It's about building everyday supports with patience, self-compassion, and a willingness to experiment. Your system is yours to shape, mix, pause, and personalize, giving you permission to find what truly works for you in each season of life. As you go forward, trust that every small effort counts. By stringing together these habits, you set up calmer mornings, lighter shoulders, and more energy left over at the end of the day—no matter how packed your calendar gets.

Conclusion

As you reach this final chapter, I want to first pause and acknowledge why you picked up this book in the first place—to find real, practical support amid the emotional whirlwind of your high-achieving life. You've made a conscious choice to take back control, and that is something worth celebrating. Remember, the entire reason for these pages has been to offer you science-driven tools not just for coping, but for transforming how you navigate the push and pull of modern demands. We began this journey with empathy, recognizing the invisible load you carry and the ways it can sneak into even the brightest days. Where chaos once dictated your emotions, you now hold a growing sense of calm and self-leadership. This is not a small feat; it's evidence of your resilience and commitment.

Looking back at everything you've explored, take a moment to appreciate how each piece fits into a larger whole. Together, we learned to notice the earliest signs of spiraling—those subtle cues in body and mind that precede overwhelm. You practiced pausing, using breath as your anchor when the world felt too loud, and trust me, those few mindful breaths really can redirect an entire day. Grounding exercises, from feeling the coolness of the floor beneath your feet to scanning your senses, showed you how to reconnect with the present when anxiety wants to sweep you away. Then came powerful mental shifts: viewing thoughts simply as information, learning not to fight them but to watch as they come and go like leaves floating by on a stream.

You've built a toolkit layer by layer—thought defusion so worries don't take center stage, gentle muscle release techniques to stave off tension before it builds, clear boundary-setting practices to protect your limited energy, and routines designed to turn these skills into lifelong habits. None of these are magic bullets, but together they form a flexible, personalized framework you can return to whenever life throws new curveballs. The beauty lies in how adaptable this approach is; you aren't expected to master everything overnight or follow a rigid script. Instead, you have the freedom to select and refine the methods that resonate best with your unique triggers, values, and schedule.

Throughout this book, some lessons may have sparked those "aha" moments—the quiet revelations that reset everything you thought you knew about emotions. Perhaps the most profound is realizing that your feelings aren't directives set in stone, but data points—signals from your inner world designed to guide, not govern, your responses. Embracing self-compassion unlocked the truth that you do not need to 'fix' your feelings or judge yourself for having them; you simply need to listen, accept, and choose your next step with kindness. For many, seeing thoughts as passing events rather than reality itself was a cornerstone shift, providing real relief from overthinking and rumination. And let's not forget the empowering act of externalizing worries—giving them shape and distance, so you can respond intentionally instead of reacting automatically. These insights make space for agency under pressure, allowing for calmer, wiser choices even in the heat of the moment.

If you've made it this far, take a deep breath and recognize the courage and dedication that brought you here. In a world that rarely slows down, carving out time to invest in your own well-being takes genuine grit. You may have started this process feeling exhausted or skeptical, but your decision to keep reading, reflecting, and practicing speaks volumes about your strength. Whether you sailed through the exercises or struggled at times, every attempt counts. You have done meaningful work by showing up for yourself repeatedly, and that effort deserves to be honored. Today, you not only understand your emotions more clearly, but you are actively shaping your mindset and behaviors in ways that support lasting growth.

This milestone is not meant to be an end point, but a launchpad for continued evolution. Every tool you've gathered becomes more effective with practice, so I encourage you to revisit favorite strategies often—perhaps setting aside regular moments to check in using the audio resources or journaling prompts we discussed. Track your progress with a habit tracker or reflect on challenging situations to see how your responses change over time. If certain patterns still feel sticky, consider reaching out for professional guidance or exploring adjacent topics like trauma-informed care or emotional intelligence at work. You're building a lifelong skill set, and there's always room to deepen, adapt, and expand.

Consider how sharing your learning can multiply its impact. By expressing what you've discovered with friends, family members, or colleagues, you model a healthier way to handle stress—breaking cycles of emotional suppression and burnout culture one honest conversation at a time. If you feel inspired, seek out or start a small group for mutual support, whether online or in person. Discussing challenges and wins together not only reinforces your growth, but also plants seeds for broader change in your community. Think of yourself as an ambassador for practical emotional regulation. The ripple effects can contribute to more compassionate workplaces, stronger relationships, and a culture where boundaries and self-care are respected rather than dismissed.

I want to close by saying thank you—truly—for inviting me along on this transformative journey. Your openness to trying new approaches, questioning old habits, and embracing vulnerability is something I never take for granted. My passion has always been to bridge solid scientific knowledge with everyday realities, making wellness accessible no matter how full your calendar or how heavy your responsibilities. Writing this book has been shaped by your stories and needs, and nothing motivates me more than knowing you've found value here. Please know that our connection doesn't have to end with these pages; if you'd like to share feedback, ask questions, or stay involved, you'll find my contact details and community platforms listed at the back. We both know that growth is ongoing—so let's keep the conversation going, together.

Reference List

3 Kind, Simple & Effective Ways to Communicate Your Boundaries | Headspace. (n.d.). Headspace for Organizations. https://organizations.headspace.com/blog/3-kind-simple-effective-ways-to-communicate-your-boundaries

Ammons, S. K. (2013, February). *Work-family boundary strategies: Stability and alignment between preferred and enacted boundaries*. Journal of Vocational Behavior. https://doi.org/10.1016/j.jvb.2012.11.002

A Realistic Guide to Time Management. (2019). Todoist Inspiration Hub. https://www.todoist.com/inspiration/time-management

Allen, D. S. (2025, May 2). *Brain Dumping: Ease Anxiety and Clear Thoughts*. Dr. Sarah Allen Counseling. https://drsarahallen.com/brain-dumping-manage-anxiety-worrying/

Amen Clinics. (2025, May 28). *5 Natural Ways to Calm Racing Thoughts | Amen Clinics Amen Clinics*. Amenclinics.com. https://www.amenclinics.com/blog/5-natural-ways-to-calm-racing-thoughts/

American Psychological Association. (2024, October 21). *Stress Effects on the Body*. American Psychological

Association; American Psychological Association. https://www.apa.org/topics/stress/body

Bobinet, K., & Greer, S. (2023, September 26). *The Iterative Mindset Method: a neuroscientific theoretical approach for sustainable behavior change and weight-loss in digital medicine.* Npj Digital Medicine; Nature Portfolio. https://doi.org/10.1038/s41746-023-00910-y

Birdee, G., Nelson, K., Wallston, K., Nian, H., Diedrich, A., Paranjape, S., Abraham, R., & Gamboa, A. (2023, May 1). *Slow breathing for reducing stress: The effect of extending exhale.* Complementary Therapies in Medicine. https://doi.org/10.1016/j.ctim.2023.102937

Burklund, L. J., Creswell, J. D., Irwin, M. R., & Lieberman, M. D. (2014, March 24). *The common and distinct neural bases of affect labeling and reappraisal in healthy adults.* Frontiers in Psychology. https://doi.org/10.3389/fpsyg.2014.00221

Bosshard, M., Guttormsen, S., Nater, U. M., Schmitz, F., Gomez, P., & Christoph Berendonk. (2025, March 12). *Improving breaking bad news communication skills through stress arousal reappraisal and worked examples.* Medical Education; Wiley. https://doi.org/10.1111/medu.15658

Balban, M. Y., Neri, E., Kogon, M. M., Weed, L., Nouriani, B., Jo, B., Holl, G., Zeitzer, J. M., Spiegel, D., & Huberman, A. D. (2023, January 10). *Brief structured respiration practices enhance mood and reduce physiological arousal.* Cell Reports Medicine. https://doi.org/10.1016/j.xcrm.2022.100895

Bentley, T. G. K., D'Andrea-Penna, G., Rakic, M., Arce, N., LaFaille, M., Berman, R., Cooley, K., & Sprimont, P. (2023, November 21). *Breathing practices for stress and anxiety reduction: Conceptual framework of implementation guidelines based on a systematic review of the published literature.* Brain Sciences. https://doi.org/10.3390/brainsci13121612

Bryant, R. A. (2021, April). *A critical review of mechanisms of adaptation to trauma: Implications for early interventions for posttraumatic stress disorder.* Clinical Psychology Review. https://doi.org/10.1016/j.cpr.2021.101981

Cognitive Defusion Techniques and Exercises. (2022). Cognitive Behavioral Therapy Los Angeles. https://cogbtherapy.com/cbt-blog/cognitive-defusion-techniques-and-exercises

Chu, B., Marwaha, K., Ayers, D., & Sanvictores, T. (2024, May 7). *Physiology, Stress Reaction.* PubMed; StatPearls Publishing. https://www.ncbi.nlm.nih.gov/books/NBK541120/

Curtiss, J. E., Levine, D. S., Ander, I., & Baker, A. W. (2021, June 17). *Cognitive-behavioral treatments for anxiety and stress-related disorders.* Focus. https://doi.org/10.1176/appi.focus.20200045

DSpace. (2025). Griffith.edu.au. https://research-repository.griffith.edu.au/bitstreams/76117508-71f5-4ecd-baf5-b2eca559fdc5/download

Endres, M., Rickert, M. E., Bogg, T., Lucas, J., & Finn, P. R. (2011, April 30). *Externalizing psychopathology and behavioral disinhibition: Working memory mediates signal discriminability and reinforcement moderates response bias in approach–avoidance learning.* Journal of Abnormal Psychology; American Psychological Association. https://doi.org/10.1037/a0022501

Eure, S. (2025, August 22). *A New Way to Understand Growth: The Iterative Mindset and What It Means for Employee Wellbeing - Fresh Tri.* Fresh Tri. https://freshtri.com/iterative-mindset-for-growth-and-employee-wellbeing/

Fincham, G. W., Kartar, A., Uthaug, M. V., Anderson, B., Hall, L., Nagai, Y., Critchley, H., & Colasanti, A. (2023, November 2). *High ventilation breathwork practices: An overview of their effects, mechanisms, and considerations for clinical applications.* Neuroscience and Biobehavioral Reviews. https://doi.org/10.1016/j.neubiorev.2023.105453

Feldhaus, C. G., Jacobs, R. H., Watkins, E. R., Peters, A. T., Bessette, K. L., & Langenecker, S. A. (2020, April 28). *Rumination-Focused Cognitive Behavioral Therapy Decreases Anxiety and Increases Behavioral Activation Among Remitted Adolescents.* Journal of Child and Family Studies. https://doi.org/10.1007/s10826-020-01711-7

Gotter, A. (2020, June 17). *Box Breathing.* Healthline. https://www.healthline.com/health/box-breathing

George, E. L. (2024, September 9). *Triggers.* MentalHealth.com. https://www.mentalhealth.com/library/understanding-triggers

Gupta, S. (2023, August 10). *Worry Time: The Benefits of Scheduling Time to Stress.* Verywell Mind. https://www.verywellmind.com/worry-time-the-benefits-of-scheduling-time-to-stress-5267979

Guenzel, N., & McChargue, D. (2023). *Addiction Relapse Prevention.* Nih.gov; StatPearls Publishing. https://www.ncbi.nlm.nih.gov/books/NBK551500/

Geneen, L. J., Moore, R. A., Clarke, C., Martin, D., Colvin, L. A., & Smith, B. H. (2017, April 24). *Physical Activity and Exercise for Chronic Pain in adults: an Overview of Cochrane Reviews.* Cochrane Database of Systematic Reviews. https://doi.org/10.1002/14651858.cd011279.pub3

Gaines, J. (2021, March 23). *How Are Habits Formed? The Psychology of Behavioral Change.* PositivePsychology.com. https://positivepsychology.com/how-habits-are-formed/

Health, M. (2025, August 8). *How to Stop Anxiety Spirals? - Axis Integrated Mental Health.* Axis Integrated Mental Health -. https://axismh.com/how-to-stop-anxiety-spirals/

Harvey, A. G., Callaway, C. A., Zieve, G. G., Gumport, N. B., & Armstrong, C. C. (2021, September 8). *Applying the science of habit formation to evidence-based psychological treatments for mental illness.* Perspectives on Psychological Science. https://doi.org/10.1177/1745691621995752

Knäuper, B., Shireen, H., Carrière, K., Frayn, M., Ivanova, E., Xu, Z., Lowensteyn, I., Sadikaj, G., Luszczynska, A., & Grover, S. (2020, January 7). *The effects of if-then plans on weight loss: results of the 24-month follow-up of the McGill CHIP Healthy*

Weight Program randomized controlled trial. Trials. https://doi.org/10.1186/s13063-019-4014-z

Le, K. (2025, June 16). *7 Best Desk-Based Exercises For Corporate Professionals.* Hyperhealth.com.au; Hyperhealth. https://www.hyperhealth.com.au/post/7-best-desk-based-exercises-for-corporate-professionals?a6f42623_page=12

Leaves on a Stream (Worksheet). (n.d.). Therapist Aid. https://www.therapistaid.com/therapy-worksheet/leaves-on-a-stream-worksheet

Morgenstern, J. (2016, March 23). *Performance under pressure, mental practice and how to use First10EM - First10EM.* First10EM. http://first10em.com/performance-under-pressure-mental-practice-and-how-to-use-first10em/

MAGNUS, A. (2025). *STOPPING COMPULSIVE RESPONSES FOR LASTING CHANGE | CONNECTION.* CONNECTION. https://innerknowing.xyz/en/post/how-to-stop-compulsive-responses-for-lasting-change/

Murphy, F., Nasa, A., Cullinane, D., Raajakesary, K., Gazzaz, A., Sooknarine, V., Haines, M., Roman, E., Kelly, L., O'Neill, A., Cannon, M., & Roddy, D. W. (2022, May 6). *Childhood Trauma, the HPA Axis and Psychiatric Illnesses: A Targeted Literature Synthesis.* Frontiers in Psychiatry. https://doi.org/10.3389/fpsyt.2022.748372

Macaulay, R., Lee, K., Johnson, K., & Williams, K. (2022, January 1). *Mindful engagement, psychological restoration, and connection with nature in constrained nature experiences.* Landscape and Urban Planning. https://doi.org/10.1016/j.landurbplan.2021.104263

Nash, J. (2018, January 5). *How to set healthy boundaries & build positive relationships.* Positive Psychology. https://positivepsychology.com/great-self-care-setting-healthy-boundaries/

NHS. (2023, January 18). *10 ways to reduce pain.* Nhs.uk. https://www.nhs.uk/live-well/pain/10-ways-to-ease-pain/

Noémie Van Maercke. (2025). *Adapt Your Spending for Summer: Creating Flexibility in Your Financial System.* Beewise Lu. https://beewiseapp.com/lu/en/adapt-your-spending-for-summer-creating-flexibility-in-your-financial-system

Nash, J. (2022, January 14). *ACT Techniques: 14 Interventions & Activities for Your Sessions.* PositivePsychology.com. https://positivepsychology.com/act-techniques/

Nursing, S. A. (2025, April 10). *Brain in Overdrive? Try this! - Straight A Nursing.* Straightanursingstudent.com. https://straightanursingstudent.com/brain-dump/

Nortje, A. (2020, July 1). *10+ best grounding techniques and exercises to strengthen your mindfulness practice today.* Positive Psychology. https://positivepsychology.com/grounding-techniques/

No Rules Just Write: A New Approach to Journaling\. (2025). Rochester.edu. https://www.urmc.rochester.edu/behavioral-health-partners/bhp-blog/april-2025/no-rules-just-write-a-new-approach-to-journaling

Neck and Jaw Stretching Exercise - University of Mississippi Medical Center. (2024). Umc.edu. https://umc.edu/ Healthcare/ENT/Patient-Handouts/Adult/Speech-Language-Pathology/Head-Neck/Neck-and-Jaw-Stretching-Exercise.html

Patwardhan, I., Nelson, T. D., McClelland, M. M., & Mason, W. A. (2021, January 6). *Childhood Cognitive Flexibility and Externalizing and Internalizing Behavior Problems: Examination of Prospective Bidirectional Associations*. Research on Child and Adolescent Psychopathology. https://doi.org/10.1007/s10802-020-00757-x

Pain Relief: Psychology, Evaluation, and Evidence-Based Interventions - David Cosio, Ph.D., ABPP. (2023). Socialworkcoursesonline.com. https:// www.socialworkcoursesonline.com/active/courses/ course141.php

Ph.D, J. S. (2024, February 2). *18 Effective Thought-Stopping Techniques (& 10 PDFs)*. PositivePsychology.com. https:// positivepsychology.com/thought-stopping-techniques/

Recovery Research Institute. (2017). *Relapse Prevention (RP) (MBRP) - Recovery Research Institute*. Recovery Research Institute. https://www.recoveryanswers.org/resource/ relapse-prevention-rp/

Routine Reset: Daily Habits for Good Mental Health | Psychology Today. (n.d.). Www.psychologytoday.com. https:// www.psychologytoday.com/us/blog/conquering-codependency/202312/routine-reset-daily-habits-for-good-mental-health

Russo, M. A., Santarelli, D. M., & O'Rourke, D. (2017, December 13). *The physiological effects of slow breathing in the healthy human.* Breathe. https://doi.org/10.1183/20734735.009817

Spreckley, M., Seidell, J., & Halberstadt, J. (2021, January 1). *Perspectives into the experience of successful, substantial long-term weight-loss maintenance: a systematic review.* International Journal of Qualitative Studies on Health and Well-Being. https://doi.org/10.1080/17482631.2020.1862481

Stinson, A. (2024). *What is box breathing?* Medical News Today. https://www.medicalnewstoday.com/articles/321805

Schuman-Olivier, Z., Trombka, M., Lovas, D. A., Brewer, J. A., Vago, D. R., Gawande, R., Dunne, J. P., Lazar, S. W., Loucks, E. B., & Fulwiler, C. (2020). *Mindfulness and Behavior Change.* Harvard Review of Psychiatry. https://doi.org/10.1097/HRP.0000000000000277

Smith, S. (2018). *5-4-3-2-1 Coping Technique for Anxiety.* Www.urmc.rochester.edu. https://www.urmc.rochester.edu/behavioral-health-partners/bhp-blog/april-2018/5-4-3-2-1-coping-technique-for-anxiety

Scott, E. (2022, December 6). *Here are ways you can journal your way out of anxiety.* Verywell Mind. https://www.verywellmind.com/journaling-a-great-tool-for-coping-with-anxiety-3144672

Sutton, J. (2022, January 2). *7 best grounding tools and techniques to manage anxiety.* PositivePsychology.com. https://positivepsychology.com/grounding-tools-techniques/

Schimming, C. (2022, March 18). *Cognitive overload: Info paralysis.* Mayo Clinic Health System; Mayo Clinic Health System. https://www.mayoclinichealthsystem.org/hometown-health/speaking-of-health/cognitive-overload

Salas Duhne, P. G., Horan, A. J., Ross, C., Webb, T. L., & Hardy, G. E. (2020, November). *Assessing and promoting the use of implementation intentions in clinical practice.* Social Science & Medicine. https://doi.org/10.1016/j.socscimed.2020.113490

Smyth, J. M., Johnson, J. A., Auer, B. J., Lehman, E., Talamo, G., & Sciamanna, C. N. (2018, December 10). *Online positive affect journaling in the improvement of mental distress and well-being in general medical patients with elevated anxiety symptoms: A preliminary randomized controlled trial.* JMIR Mental Health. https://doi.org/10.2196/11290

Schenck, L. K. (2011, September 21). *"Leaves on a Stream" - Cognitive Defusion Exercise - Mindfulness Muse.* Mindfulness Muse. https://www.mindfulnessmuse.com/acceptance-and-commitment-therapy/leaves-on-a-stream-cognitive-defusion-exercise

Tulbure, B. T., Dudău, D. P., Marian, Ş., & Watkins, E. (2025, January 2). *An internet-delivered Rumination-Focused CBT intervention for adults with depression and anxiety: A*

Randomized Controlled Trial. Behavior Therapy; Elsevier. https://doi.org/10.1016/j.beth.2024.12.004

TMJ Exercises For Pain Relief | Colgate®. (n.d.). Www.colgate.com. https://www.colgate.com/en-us/oral-health/temporomandibular-disorder/tmj-exercises-for-pain-relief

Tiba, A. I. (2024). *The grounded cognition foundation of the first cognitive model in cognitive behavior therapy: implications for practice.* Frontiers in Psychology; Frontiers Media. https://doi.org/10.3389/fpsyg.2024.1364458

Van Cappellen, P., Rice, E. L., Catalino, L. I., & Fredrickson, B. L. (2017, May 12). *Positive affective processes underlie positive health behaviour change.* Psychology & Health. https://doi.org/10.1080/08870446.2017.1320798

Wadlinger, H. A., & Isaacowitz, D. M. (2010, April 30). *Fixing Our Focus: Training Attention to Regulate Emotion.* Personality and Social Psychology Review. https://doi.org/10.1177/1088868310365565

Wieber, F., Thürmer, J. L., & Gollwitzer, P. M. (2015, July 14). *Promoting the translation of intentions into action by implementation intentions: behavioral effects and physiological correlates.* Frontiers in Human Neuroscience. https://doi.org/10.3389/fnhum.2015.00395

Yoshimura, S., Nakamura, S., & Morimoto, T. (2022, December). *Changes in neural activity during the combining affect labeling and reappraisal.* Neuroscience Research. https://doi.org/10.1016/j.neures.2022.12.001

Zulkayda Mamat, & Anderson, M. C. (2023, September 22). *Improving mental health by training the suppression of unwanted thoughts.* Science Advances; American Association for the Advancement of Science. https://doi.org/10.1126/sciadv.adh5292

jeremyp. (2024, June 6). *The Escalation Cycle of Behavior: Navigating the 7 Stages - Pollack Peacebuilding Systems.* https://pollackpeacebuilding.com/blog/behavior-escalation-cycle/

the Healthline Editorial Team. (2017, March). *Stretches to Do at Work Every Day.* Healthline; Healthline Media. https://www.healthline.com/health/deskercise

workingoncalm. (2025, May 19). *Effective Communication for Setting Boundaries Without Stress -.* Workingoncalm.com. https://workingoncalm.com/effective-communication-for-setting-boundaries-without-stress/

www.ingramcontent.com/pod-product-compliance
Lightning Source LLC
LaVergne TN
LVHW051636080426
835511LV00016B/2359